blue
rider
press

THE GUY
UNDER
THE SHEETS

ALSO BY CHRIS ELLIOTT

Into Hot Air

The Shroud of the Thwacker

Daddy's Boy

THE GUY UNDER THE SHEETS

THE UNAUTHORIZED AUTOBIOGRAPHY

Chris Elliott

BLUE RIDER PRESS

a member of Penguin Group (USA) Inc.

New York

blue
rider
press

Published by the Penguin Group
Penguin Group (USA) Inc., 375 Hudson Street, New York, New York 10014, USA •
Penguin Group (Canada), 90 Eglinton Avenue East, Suite 700, Toronto, Ontario M4P 2Y3,
Canada (a division of Pearson Penguin Canada Inc.) • Penguin Books Ltd, 80 Strand,
London WC2R 0RL, England • Penguin Ireland, 25 St Stephen's Green, Dublin 2, Ireland
(a division of Penguin Books Ltd) • Penguin Group (Australia), 250 Camberwell Road,
Camberwell, Victoria 3124, Australia (a division of Pearson Australia Group Pty Ltd) •
Penguin Books India Pvt Ltd, 11 Community Centre, Panchsheel Park, New Delhi–110 017,
India • Penguin Group (NZ), 67 Apollo Drive, Rosedale, North Shore 0632, New Zealand
(a division of Pearson New Zealand Ltd) • Penguin Books (South Africa) (Pty) Ltd,
24 Sturdee Avenue, Rosebank, Johannesburg 2196, South Africa

Penguin Books Ltd, Registered Offices: 80 Strand, London WC2R 0RL, England

Library of Congress Cataloging-in-Publication Data

Elliott, Chris, date.
The guy under the sheets : the unauthorized autobiography / Chris Elliott.
p.   cm.
ISBN 978-0-399-15840-7
1. Elliott, Chris, date.   2. Actors—United States—Biography.   3. Comedians—United States—
Biography.   4. Authors, American—21st century—Biography.   I. Title.
PN2287.E42A3   2012   2012027261
791.4302'8092—dc23
[B]

Printed in the United States of America
1   3   5   7   9   10   8   6   4   2

BOOK DESIGN BY MEIGHAN CAVANAUGH

For David Rosenthal.

It is only because of his vigorous and ultimately successful efforts to surmount the blockades erected by Chris Elliott's attorneys that this important work could finally be published.

In Elliott's work we see the archetypal comedic hero turned upside down. He not only confounds the ethical and social conception that comedy must be "funny" to be entertaining—but he even goes as far as to confound the high-brow notion that "non-funny" comedy must be "non-funny" for a reason, and not just the accidental result of having no talent and no idea what you're doing. . . . In that sense, he is very much the poor man's Andy Kaufman. The very, very poor man's Andy Kaufman.

—PIERRE BOURDIEU, *Distinction: A Social Critique of the Judgment of Taste*

THE GUY
UNDER
THE SHEETS

ONE

It was November 10, 1982, and Studio 6A was the place to be. That night as usual it was packed to capacity, the audience bubbling with the kind of antsy anticipation usually reserved for NBC megastars like Willard Scott. A comic revolution was in the air, and back then the fans who *got* it, and the curious who *wanted* to get it, as well as those who *thought* they got it but were afraid of being caught *not* getting it, all flocked to Rockefeller Center to experience a live taping of the new hit show *Late Night with David Letterman*. (Or at least the ones who couldn't get tickets to *Saturday Night Live*, or the Christmas Show at Radio City Music Hall, or the Roller Derby, or pretty much anything else.)

Fidgeting nervously in their seats, the crowd desperately searched the stage for a glimpse of the man they had come to see—the man whose midwestern charm, irreverent style, and cool Girbaud snap-ankle pants were causing more than just a little stir in the stodgy middle-of-the-road clam chowder called "network television." David Braumstein Letterman was a mere fifty-nine years old at the time, but already a megastar. *Late Night* had premiered only a few months before but was already one of NBC's top raters, bettered only by the controversial prime-time talk show *The Truman Capote Kiss My Sweet White Ass Hour*—in which, predictably, the drunken host would invite his weary guests to do just that.

On this night, Dave waited backstage, savoring the moment. He had come a long way from the plywood shed in Indianapolis, where he'd spent his days "noodling" catfish and feeling up soft-serve operators behind the old Piggly Wiggly. Primping before a full-length mirror, he straightened his tie, scuffed up his wrestling shoes, and replaced his bridge with the same gap-toothed character teeth that had made the kids shriek when he appeared at 4H events as the dim-witted Horseface Willie, back in his summer-job days.

"Everybody had some sort of gimmick back then," Letterman told *Dental World* magazine in 1990. "Minnie Pearl had her 'How-dee' thing, Skelton crossed his eyes, and my pal Brokaw always delivered the news with a bunch of marbles in his mouth, so I figured I needed a gimmick, too. And by golly, but those smelly kids on the farms sure loved my funny fake teeth. Why, they would just howl at the mere sight of them. Land o' Goshen, how they would howl!"

By now the audience was stamping its feet. Bill Wendell, a tall man with an equally tall hairpiece (which played host to a frightful assemblage of chiggers, ticks, and cracker crumbs), stood at the ready in front of his trusty NBC microphone. He narrowed his eyes on the restless audience and stuck his fingers in his ears to block out the cacophony. A veteran of television and radio, Wendell thought he had seen it all, but tonight he was forced to admit that something different was in the air. *Late Night* had struck a nerve with the disillusioned youth of America—who were especially disillusioned at the time, mainly because there wasn't anything much to be disillusioned about (except for their realization that sitcoms weren't real?).

Dave had cast himself as the master of ceremonies for a wacky circus of eccentric guests, cutting-edge comedy, and stupid pet tricks, but he especially enjoyed showcasing the occasional ham-headed staff member in comedy bits that were uncomfortable and humiliating. Dave and his audience took perverse pleasure in watching these novice entertainers squirm and stumble their way through inept performances. Yet, ironically, some of these neophytes were beginning to garner followings of their own. Tonight, in fact, Dave would surrender the spotlight to one especially ham-headed young staff member—a certain bald, bearded ne'er-do-well from the tough neighborhoods of the posh Upper East Side, whose special brand of ineptness was about to launch him into a career more uncomfortable and humiliating than anything in his wildest dreams.

Stage manager Biff Henderson strolled into the studio looking slightly skittish. He was shaking off another Pleiku flashback—this one involving a bamboo cage, Russian roulette, and the capuchin monkeys he claimed held him captive for ten years in Nam. He raised his hand and began to count down, "Five, four, three, two, one." Paul Shaffer hit the first chords of the opening theme and the crowd went crazy. You could barely hear Wendell announce: "It's *Late Night with David Letterman*! Tonight, Dave's guests include Brother Theodore, comedian Gary Mule Deer, Dr. Ruth Westheimer, money guru Matthew Lesko, the curator of the Tissue Paper Museum, plus stupid pet tricks, elevator races, and . . . a new running character starring our own Chris Elliott!"

At that moment something unusual, perhaps even magical, happened. In response to hearing Elliott's name, the audience exploded with yelps and screams, and one woman fainted straightaway. Then the crowd went positively berserk. The bleachers shook and the catwalk above rattled so violently that one of the obese grips lost his balance and fell forty feet to his death—killing another obese grip who was standing below him. (Their names have been lost to history, but who cares? They were *obese*.)

And although it turned out later that this was all just because some nutcase had let his pet squirrel loose in the audience, at the time it seemed that the words "Chris Elliott" had suddenly acquired star power. Backstage, the writers and producers who were gathered around the monitor pricked up their ears and exchanged baffled looks. In terms of hierarchy, twenty-one-year-old Elliott was a low man on the totem pole, to say the least (and also not the swiftest mop in the mudroom). Up in the offices, he was just a guy Friday, spending most of his time running numbers, hitting on chicks, and pissing in the coffeemaker. He'd been on the show several times before—once as a talking pile of garbage—and he even had a few underdog-loving fans of his own, including this one priest who kept calling NBC to offer his services as an exorcist, but at this point, honestly, Dave's desk was getting more fan mail.

Letterman, slightly baffled, made his entrance and shot off a couple of winners about canned hams and after-dinner mints, and then sat down and proceeded with the show. Everything went as planned. The audience responded warmly, if a tad moderately, to the grab bag of off-the-wall guests and stunt comedy . . . until it came time for Elliott's appearance. Reading from one of his ubiquitous blue cards, Dave said, "Ladies and gentlemen, it's time for the first episode of a new running character starring our own—" Suddenly it happened again. The audience went absolutely insane, and a woman in the back screamed, "I think it ran up my leg!"

"Seriously?" Dave muttered to himself. "For that chucklehead? The hell with this. Let's just bring him out. Ladies and gentlemen, please welcome the Guy Under the Seats!"

Below the bleachers, only Elliott was oblivious to the mayhem above. He was in the midst of attempting another "knee-knocker"— his nickname for stand-up sex, which he regularly indulged in before any appearance on the show, even if no one was handy to do it with him. He was superstitious that way, and the show was so popular that there was usually some faceless groupie or nameless industry girl or especially attractive mop head hanging around backstage who was more than happy to oblige him in the hopes of getting an official *Late Night* collapsible cup or a facial blotter, or just a chance to meet Dave's desk.

"Please welcome *the Guy Under the Seats*," Dave repeated, now visibly competing with the crowd's deafening squeals.

Biff Henderson ran under the bleachers. "That's your cue!" he shouted. "Don't you hear the audience? They're going crazy for you! Now get out there! That's your cue, damn it!" He yanked Elliott off the groupie—whom he immediately recognized. "Oh, excuse me," he said.

"Vot in hell is a 'facial blotter'?" asked Dr. Ruth Westheimer, steadying herself on wobbly legs. (She may have been a bit confused, but she would have been totally satisfied had Biff not interrupted.)

5

Elliott snapped at Biff, "How dare you! You know this is my private time!" Then he threw a hard right at the stage manager's jaw, which would have sent the man flying, had Chris possessed anything resembling strength or coordination. (As it was, Biff just thought Elliott was having some kind of arm spasm.) Chris turned back to Westheimer. "Sorry, baby," he purred, and stuffed a facial blotter in her blazer pocket. "We'll have to continue our interesting discussion about those pesky fallopian tubes some other time. Right now, I have to go dazzle the folks with some of my *other* talents." Then he gallantly kissed her hand, gave her his best Jack Lord wink, and disappeared up a ladder, while Dr. Ruth stormed off shouting, "Vo ist mine lawyer?"

Up above, a hatch blew open and a blast of confetti shot up to the rafters. When it cleared, Elliott was standing there in all his glory. "Hello, all," he said in a sultry, come-hither-and-tell-me-all-your-deepest-darkest-desires voice, which was almost lost in the noise of the hyped-up throng.

In 1991, Elliott's first biographer (who committed suicide halfway through the process) recounted the moment as follows:

> It was sheer pandemonium. Elliott just stood there motionless soaking it all in—his initial look of erotic defiance replaced with a dopey, wide-eyed mystification that seemed to say, "What did I do this time?" Shirtless, exuding raw, unadulterated middle-aged masculinity (although he was only twenty-one at the time and not particularly masculine), the light danced on his fake beard, and the mangy wisps of blond hair on top of his egg-shaped head fluttered in the breeze like insect antennae. His sinewy muscles—virtually nonexistent— hung from his arms like melting white chocolate, and his round

pectorals bounced about like big bags of pudding. He was covered in clammy perspiration, which made him appear even sexier—to himself. . . . Oh, what the hell is the point in going on with this shit? I thought writing a biography would be a nice change of pace, but I can't take this moron anymore. I'm going to put myself to sleep now for a bit longer than usual. Call it eternity.

—Jerzy Kosinski, 1991

A viewing of one of the few surviving grainy Kinescopes of the show confirms Kosinski's observations. In it one sees ghostly images of a frenzied mob, clambering wildly on top of one another, criss-crossing in front of the cameras, and in some cases even being bodily restrained and beaten by NBC security guards.

What followed was classic Letterman–Elliott repartee, although you can barely hear it over the pops and clicks on the old telerecording:

DAVE: Hi, Chris, we haven't seen you for a while. Where have you been?

CHRIS: I've been living under the seats, Dave. It's my new running character.

DAVE: Oh, great, and what exactly happens with the character?

CHRIS: What?

DAVE: I say, what exactly happens with this character?

CHRIS: Oh, well, I climb out from under the seats and I say, "Hi, Dave," and then I climb back down until the next time.

DAVE: That's it?

CHRIS: Essentially.

DAVE: Okay, well, thanks.

CHRIS: What?

DAVE: I said, thanks.

CHRIS: Okay.

As Whitney Balliett so aptly wrote in *The New Yorker*: "When the two were in sync it was like sweet jazz." He was talking about Thelonious Monk and Dizzy Gillespie, but the same could be said of Elliott and Letterman, theoretically. At their best they were like Nichols and May, or Burns and Allen, and at their worst they were still moderately better than the Hudson Brothers (remember them, folks?).

Then Chris went back below the seats, the squirrel made another break for it, and the crowd went wild again. Authentic or not, the reaction was contagious. Those nowhere near the epicenter just assumed they weren't getting the joke and cheered even louder to cover for it. Within moments Chris had a pack of newly minted diehard fans, all chanting, "El-liott! El-liott!"

"I just don't get it," said Biff to Wendell. "Is there something in the water?"

"Maybe it's the beard," Wendell replied, picking a grub out of his hairpiece. "Do you think I should grow one?"

"I guess he was funny in some way I'm too old to get," Biff postulated.

"Nah, what's funny is that it's not funny. It's the new thing. Like you know with that guy . . . what's-his-name, from *Taxi*."

"Whatever the reason, they love him now," Letterman said, returning backstage and spitting his buck teeth into a glass of soda water. "Which means, from now on I'm going to have to find some other stooge to clean my bidet, tee-hee-hee."

Dave could not have been more right. (At least about the audience loving Chris, but Chris would actually retain all bidet-related responsibilities until 1985, when Dave finally shelled out for one of the new Japanese self-cleaning models.) "The Guy Under the Seats" was in fact destined to become one of the most beloved running characters performed by a relative unknown on a TV show watched mostly by socially isolated insomniacs in our nation's history. Elliott had touched a nerve with his audience and showed them something they could relate to, a working-class schlub with no talent and no chin, struggling against the man for his own little piece of the limelight.

As Frank Rich would later write in *The New York Times* (during one of those Augusts when nothing else was happening): "Elliott has finally broken through. No longer will he be viewed as a mere idiot, but as a blue-collar idiot, the kind of idiot that America loves—and fears. . . . He's leading his own one-man insurgency against the *avant-garde*, nailing a message to the door of those so-called 'conceptual comedians,' a message that says, 'I don't need your stupid concepts. I don't even need to bathe regularly. . . .' Clearly that snob Andy Kaufman could learn a thing or two from him."

Exactly what Andy Kaufman—then the reigning king of "not-funny funny"—thought of all this has long been a subject of debate. He rarely deigned to speak of Elliott in interviews, though he once offered to wrestle him, but only if it could be to the death. "In fact," as he told *Big Bulging Eyes* magazine, "I may just hire someone to have that sellout killed. . . . You can't tell if I'm joking, can you? That's how clever I am!"

He wasn't alone in his animosity. For every person who adored Elliott, there were at least two more who would have liked to see him floating belly-up in the fishbowl of fame. Partly this was the inevitable result of having finally made it into the spotlight, but mostly it was just him. Although all his characters were weirdly human, or weird humans, and thus relatable to most everybody, especially shut-ins, there was something of himself in all of them, something of his most true and hidden nature—and that was the problem. No one was sure exactly *what* that nature was, because very little he did actually made any sense. Was "The Panicky Guy" an expression of the dislocation felt by modern man in a world without any clear social or moral landmarks, or had Chris just been popping too many pep pills that morning? Was "The Fugitive Guy" a polished pearl of a postmodern pièce de résistance, or had he just been up all night watching Quinn Martin reruns desperately looking for something to steal? (To say nothing of his beloved "Marlon," which many have speculated was just the result of an allergic reaction to bananas.) In short, was he a Chauncey Gardiner (or a Forrest Gump, for our younger readers), an innocent simpleton stumbling through the corrupt and decadent world of televised entertainment, reflecting its contradictions while remaining mysteriously untouched . . . or was he just a spoiled kid desperate to capture the tiniest piece of our collective attention by any—and I do mean *any*—means necessary?

In order to attempt to answer these questions, we must go through his life chronologically and in excruciating detail, at least for long enough to fill about two hundred pages, most of which will have to be padded with a lot of childhood anecdotes and pop-psych speculation. (I've hired an expert.) But first we should probably just finish the teaser.

After the show that night, Chris stumbled through a gauntlet of writers, producers, and dangerously obsessed fans, now all suddenly eager to congratulate or stalk him: "Right on, brother," said Biff. "Fabulous," cooed Paul Shaffer, knuckling him on the chin. Dave threw an arm around his shoulder and said, "I got to hand it to you, kid, you've got chutzpah. You give me great nachas." Even Dr. Ruth—who had been playing it so coy earlier—seemed to suddenly warm up to him. "Perhaps I von't be pressing charges, after all," she said, kissing him on the cheek, then adding under her breath, "*Was für ein Mann.* I swear, if it's the last thing I do, I'm going to make him mine."

Needless to say, Chris was baffled, mainly because he was baffled by just about everything, even the inner workings of a paper cup, but also because he had no idea what he'd done to make people like him—and, more importantly, no idea how to do it again. If he'd been smart (he wasn't, but if he had been), he would have been terrified of blowing it, of being revealed as a phony, a fake, a charlatan, a fraud—of living the rest of his life plagued by the knowledge that he was pretending to be something he was not. But, knowing him, he was probably just thinking about his extensive collection of Gobots.

He retreated from the throng, blowing kisses, bowing, winking, mouthing, "I love you all," until he made it to the relative safety of the mop closet that doubled as his dressing room. He closed the door behind him, kicked aside the wheelie bucket, and made room for himself on the mud sink in front of his makeshift makeup mirror. "What the hell just happened?" he said to himself, then added, "Maybe I should get a chin implant."

Suddenly there was a knock at his door. "Special delivery," said a voice. Chris opened the door to reveal a courier who handed him a bouquet of lilies and a large box with a glitzy star-shaped bow.

"A congratulations gift!" he cried. "How nice! This must be what it's like to be famous now. Maybe there's a pretty girl inside." He untied the beautiful tulle ribbon and opened the box. Inside, wrapped unceremoniously in some old newspaper, he found a boiled lobster with a card attached to it. He froze. His eyes glazed over, and he began to shake uncontrollably. He didn't have to read the card. He knew all too well the terrifying implications of the dead-shellfish-gram and from whom the message had been sent. Nevertheless, slowly . . . sheepishly . . . and wishing he had the strength to stop himself, he opened the card and read:

Congratulations, faker!

> *Your loving mother,*
> *Bette Davis*

TWO

I n the 1960s, the Elliott family lived on Manhattan's Upper East Side. With its pristine, tree-lined blocks and quaint caviar pushcarts, it was considered one of the safest and most respectable neighborhoods in all of New York. However, this sanitized perception could not have been further from the truth. Under its well-perfumed exterior was a volatile, perilous battleground. The turbulence of the decade had reached even this last bastion of old-school urban civility—although here the problem wasn't the youth clashing with the establishment as much as the establishment clashing with itself. It was the classic struggle "old money versus new," which, along with "fat versus skinny," "hot versus cold," and "bad versus it's okay but still not that great," would become profound themes in the future works of Chris Elliott—who, though not yet born, was practically knocking at the front door, if you know what I mean. In fact, by 1961 he was already halfway out, and had been that way for about six months, though it would take another year of heated debate and legal wrangling before his parents finally decided to make him official. Subconsciously, Elliott never fully forgave his mother and father for this period of indecision, and for the rest of his life he was plagued by horrible nightmares in which he saw himself drowning whenever his mother took a bath.

The old money families had dominated the Upper East Side of Manhattan for centuries, holding sway over fashionable dinner parties, debutante balls, and rodent hunts, but now they faced competition from a new set of families who weren't born into money but had instead amassed their fortunes by using the William Morris agency to land themselves lucrative sweetheart deals. The old money deeply resented these usurpers, whose wealth had grown steadily ever since the Depression, and even more steadily now since the Madoffs had moved into the area. Old-money and new-money gangs roamed the streets, hurling crude affronts and savage indignities at one another.

Chris's block was the epicenter for this conflict. The south side of the street belonged to the old vanguard—the Vanderbilts, Astors, and Borgias, while the north side was the sole domain of the new blood—the Liberaces, the Tom Carvels, and the Elliotts themselves. Although both sides were rich, the old money was richer. In fact, the Borgias were so old and so rich that they could actually hire the new money to do some of their insulting for them, which of course was counterproductive because it meant that the new money just ended up insulting themselves. The discord escalated until a clear line of demarcation was drawn between both sides—originally in white paint, but green on St. Patrick's Day, and silver whenever Liberace threw a block party. Peaceful afternoons were often shattered by the shrill sounds of air-raid sirens as the opposing gangs faced off with one another, giving boisterous flight to their hateful slurs.

It was impossible to grow up in such an environment without getting drawn into the conflict. Everyone had to take sides, and often it was brother against brother, nanny against butler, wife against mistress, or, in the case of the Elliotts, parents against children. Young Chris, during a rebellious period, briefly pledged into The Blue Ascots, the Auchincloss gang, and was working his way up to junior footwarmer when his mother finally caught him up in his bedroom trying to cut toast points out of a loaf of homemade "pinch me" bread.

"It's bad enough you had to be born!" she cried, covering her eyes in shame. "Did you have to add insult to injury?"

Bette Davis of course had never wanted to be a mother. She'd never wanted to be anything but a famous actress. Born in Lowell, Massachusetts, in 1908, she'd known she was destined for stardom since the age of five, when she saw a production of *Julius Caesar* in a neighbor's backyard, starring Spanky McFarland and Darla Hood— with a cameo by Billie "Buckwheat" Thomas. "I knew right then and there that I could be the next Darla if I wanted to be," she told Walter Winchell. "But those little rascals were jealous of my wealthy father and wouldn't let me join their gang. I think Darla was intimidated by me, to be honest with you." Of course it didn't help matters much when Bette dragged Darla's boyfriend, Alfalfa, behind the barn and popped his cherry so hard his cowlick went limp. Fortunately for him he had powerful friends, and the Lowell Elementary School teacher, Miss Crabtree, immediately expelled little Bette Davis and sent Alfalfa to the hospital to have his cherry discreetly reattached.

Soon after, Bette traveled to Hollywood, where her big beautiful Bambi eyes (which she'd stolen from an actual baby deer) and her tempestuous personality appealed to movie producers and audiences alike. She was just what the Depression-era gay community was looking for (i.e., a good reason not to regret having left their domineering fake wives and moved to LA). She quickly became one of the biggest stars of all time, applauded both for her willingness to play villainous characters and for her scrupulous attention to realism. When she played Mr. Freeze, she even shaved her head and eyebrows, and never once during shooting did she take off the fake muscle suit that the wardrobe people had constructed for her out of one of the cured skins that Schwarzenegger sheds after a wax and tan. (This professionalism had a profound impact on Chris, who shaved his head for his role in James Cameron's The Abyss. Unfortunately, his hair never grew back.)

But then came the summer of '59, when Bette first laid eyes on the man who would become Chris's father—the gun-slinging, meat-lovin', rope-twirling Western actor and social critic Sam Elliott. (Some of you may have heard that Chris's dad was Bob Elliott, of the popular comedy team Bob and Ray, but Bob Elliot is actually the famous father of hip-hop vocalist Missy Elliott. It's a common mistake.) At the time Bette was married to actor Gary Merrill and living in their beloved Witch Way cottage, next door to Frank Sinatra's beloved My Way ranch, and right outside Maine's beloved Boothbay Harbor. The Merrill-Davis marriage was a tumultuous one to say the least, but the two seemed devoted to each other despite their combative egos. That all changed, however, on the night of August 6, when Bette saw Sam doing his famous "Slow Rope-Twirlers of America" routine at the Ogunquit Playhouse.

"I was immediately attracted to the combination of masculinity, musk, and simple-minded genius," Bette told Hedda Hopper. "He exuded all four. Although to be perfectly honest, the musk and simple-mindedness seemed to dominate—a warning sign to which I admit that I should have paid more attention."

For his part, Sam was also immediately attracted. It was like he was hit by a bolt of lightning, and when he spoke with *Raw Hide* magazine in 1962, he was obviously still consumed by passion, and unable to contain his buoyant, childlike enthusiasm: "I just wanted a cigarette," he said. "I was out of Camels and I really needed a smoke."

Bette immediately divorced Gary Merrill, and Sam divorced his first wife, Joan Crawford, and the two went back to New York City, got married, and began setting up house at San Semolina, the twelve-story Gothic mansion that had once served as the final holdout for the Knights Templar, after the city was sacked by the Ottoman Empire in 1312. Unfortunately, however, within a year things had already begun to sour. There was trouble in paradise, a fly in the ointment, a snake in the garden, and although they could overlook most of these annoying infestations—this *was* New York City, after all—they couldn't ignore the wild hair up their respective asses. Two extremely competitive, egomaniacal actors do not a happy family make, and they were constantly at each other's throats.

But by the time they realized they'd made a mistake it was already too late. They had already made the holes in the sheets speak the language of love. Bette was knocked up, and this being before *Roe v. Wade*, she had to rely on the then-popular but not very effective do-it-yourself method of taking hot gin baths while freebasing Vicks VapoRub. It cleared her sinuses but had little effect on her tubes.

The birth was difficult for Bette, not just because she hated failing at anything, but also because she was not one to sit idly by and let any so-called medical professionals do the work for her. The poor midwives found themselves chasing her all over the delivery room, refilling her schnapps glass, lighting her cigarettes, and enduring her hourly tirades—all while imploring her to "relax, breathe, and push."

"'Relax, breathe, and push'?" she barked back, her hands on her hips in that classic Bette Davis pose. "Who the hell do you think you're talking to? I've never relaxed, breathed, or pushed one god-damn day in my whole goddamn life, and I don't plan on starting now! If this kid or whatever the hell it is wants to pop out of me, that's his business—not mine. And I better not catch any of you spanking him to life, either. If he wants to breathe, he'll have to learn the same way I did—from Humphrey Bogart."

And so into this chaotic, mixed-up family, little "Bulbousnoggen" was born. A week later his name was shortened to Chris—after the umbilical cord that had "accidentally" gotten wrapped around his neck was finally removed and his cranium had shrunk down to a normal size. After another week, however, it shrank even more, and as a joke Bette and Sam legally changed his name to "Raisinnoggen," but the boy always preferred to be called Chris, or Cliff, or even Paper Clip if you couldn't remember Cliff or Chris.

He was a beautiful, gentle, somewhat sickly child with two club-feet, buckteeth, and a hand growing out of his stomach. He was also blessed with the ability to drool about a quart of saliva a day. From an early age, Chris displayed a marked interest in all forms of life, even the smallest, most insignificant forms of life, like jockeys and Danny DeVito. He once cried hysterically when his mother crushed a water bug under her heel. Sam felt bad and bought him a water bug farm and Chris spent hours and hours just staring at the thing.

Eventually Bette had enough and sprayed the farm with Raid. He never forgave her for this wanton act of cruelty.

Chris couldn't tolerate the killing of any living creature, even for food. He and his little mates often rescued live lobsters from the local fish market and flushed them down the toilet, reasoning that they'd somehow find their way back to the ocean. When Sam explained to him that they were probably dying horribly slow and excruciating deaths in a septic tank somewhere, Chris was so despondent that he took his next rescue home and raised it in a pail under his bed. He named it Snappy, and he loved it so much that he would even beg his parents to let it sit at the dinner table with him.

Often Bette would plead with Sam to put his foot down. He could be an intimidating man when he wanted to be, and his feet could be even more intimidating when they wanted to be. A thick mane of salt-and-pepper hair crowned his larger-than-life head, and his chiseled Rushmore-like face was adorned with a set of wild, intimidating eyebrows and a larger-than-life intimidating mustache. At six feet tall, he cast a long shadow—a shadow that he was determined that young Chris would learn to walk in. In fact, he was so determined that he hired a stand-in to cast a shadow for him so that Chris could practice whenever Sam was away traveling the country, twirling rope, or making astute observations about everyday life—like his famous one-liner "Meat. It's what's for dinner," and his ubiquitous catchphrase "If mankind can't get along, then I say get along little doggies, get along," and of course his oft-quoted "Tough titties, said the kitty, but the milk's still good—if you like cat milk, which I do, and I'm famous, so now you have to buy it. (*Drink MeowMeow*)." The fact that most of his "astute observations" made virtually no sense whatsoever was lost on the intellectual elite, who saw quiet brilliance in everything he did, even the quiet, brilliant way he scratched his balls with a shoehorn. In fact, his "classic" essay lampooning the IHOP restaurant chain—titled "Stack 'Em High, Baby, 'Cause I Got Miles to Eat Before I Sleep"—won a Pulitzer Prize in folksiness, and went on to be included in Harvard's prestigious "five-foot shelf of knowledge."

"Now, listen here, little pardner," Sam would tell Chris. "Pigs and chickens are one thing, but where I come from nothing that chews with its hands is allowed to sit at the table."

"But Snappy says he can't help how he eats. Isn't that right, Snappy?" said Chris, putting his head close to Snappy's claws to hear the reply, and then screaming and running in circles when the lobster inevitably attached itself to his earlobe.

"It would almost be funny," Bette would say, pouring herself another schnapps, "if this weren't like the fourth time this has happened . . . *today*."

Obviously, Chris was not a bright boy. Sometimes after dinner, while Sam and Bette sat up counting references to themselves on TV, Chris would stand behind the set holding a pencil and his little Brownie camera. "What in the heckfire tarnation do you think yer do'n back there, you dumb pecker-pole?" Sam Elliott would lovingly ask. Chris would smile slyly like he knew something that no one else in the world could possibly know. "I'm waiting for the little actors to come out the stage door," he would say, "so I can get their autographs." And then he would clap his hands and jump up and down, and sing like an imbecile.

Sam did his best to toughen the boy up, taking him on fishing trips at the aquarium, hunting trips at the zoo, and drag nights at My

Mama's Hat Box. These were meaningful father-son bonding experiences for Chris, though he later found out that they hadn't been with his father at all, but with one of his stand-ins. Sam employed dozens of look-alikes, mostly as stunt doubles on his Westerns, but some also stood in for him on the home front, helping out with the household chores, PTA meetings, and even making angry love to his old lady—just like Sam himself, only angrier.

Sadly, it turned out Chris had actually been bonding with a guy named Jim Bailey (who incidentally did an amazing Dionne Warwick at the Box). His real father had grown so sick of Bette's relentless "blusteration" ("bullshit" to you and me) that he'd long since contrived to be away from home for most of Chris's natural life. Obviously this must have been a traumatic revelation for the boy, the effects of which would be impossible for anyone to imagine without the aid of some fancy degree. Fortunately, we have the insights of Dr. Amelia Adler, the noted psychologist and Elliottology specialist, who was more than happy to be interviewed for this book. (Apparently there aren't a lot of jobs in Elliottology these days.)

> With his father away twirling god-knows-whose mustache on the end of his rope, and his mother preoccupied with makeup tests for *Whatever Happened to Baby Jane?*, young Chris was compelled to turn inward for solace and support. Like many "creative types," he made up for his lack of strength and masculinity with an excess of sensitivity, developing what is sometimes called an ISFP type personality (introverted, sensing, feeling, and perceiving), but which is more commonly known as the LLPB type personality, or the Light in the Loafers Pansy Boy personality, the sort who gets on everyone's nerves

talking about how gorgeous sunsets are until you just want to kick him in the ass, if you know what I mean (swish-swish).

Each day Chris would walk home from school dressed in his favorite outfit of blue shorts, blue blazer, and woman's bouffant wig (the same look he would later adopt for *Cabin Boy*), his mind wandering as he traipsed through the lilies in the park or giggled at the antics of his local firemen, seemingly oblivious to the sights and sounds of the real-life rough-and-tumble city. Around him car horns honked, dogs barked, sirens wailed, and blood-curdling screams curdled blood, while the noisy street vendors—the fishmongers, the meatmongers, and the warmongers—cried their wares.

And yet without realizing it, he must have been subconsciously absorbing the local characters around him, squirreling them away for later retrieval. There was nervous old Mr. Angelini, who always seemed to be in a state of total panic about one thing or another. "Oh my God, the Chicago fire started back up and it's heading for New York! I gotta get out of here. I gotta get out of here!"

There was also shifty-eyed old Mr. Koratzanis in his baggy pants and wingtip shoes, who saw conspiracies around every street corner. "Hey, kid, did you hear the Chicago fire started up again and it's heading for New York? It's a conspiracy, I'm telling you. I gotta get out of here! I gotta get out of here!"

And there was Roger Cambell, who never told anybody where he was from. "Oh, you know . . . here, there. All around, really." Every other day he seemed to hold a different occupation.

And finally there was the old black Con Edison man, who would pop up from under the street through various manholes. And stand half underground, half in the real world, his lower extremities hidden beneath the asphalt. There he would chat with his fellow work-ers or eat his lunch, or whistle at the passing chicks, and when it came time to get back to work, he would retreat down to his myste-rious domain, closing the lid above him.

He was by far Chris's favorite. Chris called him "The Guy Under the Streets" and even stopped sometimes to listen to him ramble—along with a handful of other clued-in seven-year-olds in the neigh-borhood, who weren't satisfied with the sanitized conventional wisdom being spoon-fed to them by the mostly white, *aboveground* Con Edison workers. Guy Under the Streets was the real deal—the genuine black, *belowground*, manhole-*dweller* experience. He was like the difference between whole wheat and Wonder bread, between a Harley and a moped, between leather pants and Sansabelt slacks, and it was he who gave Chris the single most crucial piece of advice of his early years:

"Ditch the wig, kid," he said. "It makes you look like a damn girl."

But Chris protested. The wig was obviously his way of debas-ing himself on behalf of womankind, "because, you know, women have been debased for like forever, so now it's, uh, like us guys' turn . . ."

"Yeah, well, I don't go much for that fancy Harvard sociology talk. Down in the tunnels life is simple. It's just a man, his waders, his headlamp, and maybe a sandwich, walking the fine line of the underside. And from here all I see is a boy who really needs to get his pipes cleaned, if you know what I mean."

Chris didn't, but the man's words reverberated in his mind for days afterward. (It's hard to know what kind of physical effect that sort of continuous reverberation could have on a little brain, but obviously it didn't help matters much up there.)

Young Chris started behaving oddly, especially around holes in things, or things that were under other things. He began to pay special attention to basements, exhaust pipes, and culverts. He was banned from the locker room after he greased himself up and slipped down an eight-inch shower drain just to see what the tile smelled like on the inside. He started spending a lot of time in his room, staying up into the wee hours of the morning pacing his floor and talking to Snappy, making secret plans. He asked Jim Bailey for some tools—a saw, some lumber, and a twenty-foot-tall extension ladder, but when Jim asked what it was all for, Chris would only say, "You'll know when the revolution comes."

Then it finally happened. There are many accounts as to what exactly went down that day, but we'll take the testimony of Desideria Vargas, the Elliotts' housekeeper (mainly because hers was the cheapest):

Ms. Davis came flying into the room, because she heard Master Chris calling for her, but when she got there, there was nobody.

"Where's the idiot gone to now?" she asked. Then a trapdoor in the middle of the oriental carpet opened up and Master Chris popped his head out.

"Hi, Ma!" he said. His face was covered in shoe polish and he was wearing a hard hat with the words CON EDISON on it.

"May I ask just what in the hell you think you're doing?"

"I'm the Guy Under the Oriental Carpet."

"And who is that, the village idiot?"

"No, it's a *bit*."

"A bit of what?"

"Like for a show," Chris explained.

"Who's your talent rep, son? Santa Claus?"

"Uh . . ." Chris was too young to really know what a talent rep was, so he just stuck to the book. "You see, I come out, make observations, then I go back in."

"That's it? It'll never sell. You've got no Act Two, plus it's asinine."

"Okay, uh . . . bye now."

He tried to go back down the trapdoor, but Bette stopped it with her foot, kicked it back open, and bent down over him.

"Do you have any idea how much that rug cost me?"

"You said it was a gift from Howard Hughes."

"I meant spiritually! Now go to your room until I decide what to do with you!"

According to Desideria, Chris was sent to bed without his supper. But apparently he began to moan and cry out that he was starving, and that his belly had swollen from lack of protein, and that he was starting to have visions of angels on fence posts, even though it was only about four-thirty in the afternoon and only about a half-hour after his snack time, so Bette finally let him come down to the table.

"But you have to promise to be on your best behavior! No nonsense, no stupidity. In fact, no talking in general."

Chris promised, and sat down obediently while Bette, now made up in her casual dinnertime Jane Hudson look, went to work at the stove. But within a few moments the little boy was shifting in his seat.

"What? What is it now?" said Bette, taking the lid off a pot of boiling water.

"Can Snappy come to the table, too?"

"Did you hear that, honey?" Bette said to Jim Bailey, who was standing in for Sam that night. "He wants to know if Snappy can come to the table."

"Yeah, that's a good one, all right," voiced Jim, who was in full Dionne Warwick drag but sounded just like Sam. "Real funny."

Bette laughed heartily, then reached for a paper bag.

"What?" asked Chris. "What's so funny?"

"Nothing, nothing at all," Bette replied. Then, to Jim, added, "Honey, would you mind melting us a stick of butter?"

It took a while for the realization to dawn, Chris being Chris. His first clue was the shell cracker by Jim's plate. His second clue was the lobster bib tied around his neck. His third clue was the writhing paper bag Bette was suddenly holding over the pot.

"What's going on?" Chris inquired.

"Would you care to do the honors?" Bette asked Jim.

"Look, little buddy," Jim said, examining his mascara in a compact mirror. "Your mother and I have been talkin', and we've decided it's time for you to grow up and face some facts."

Bette cackled. "Yeah, like (a) lobsters are for eating, (b) rugs are for standing on, and (c) you will never be good at anything, ever."

"Wait," said Chris. "You mean we're eating . . . *Snappy*?"

"That's our little genius," Bette quipped.

"Must take after your side of the family."

Chris cried out, "Please, Mom, don't do it!"

"Pop goes the weasel," she snarled, and with that she dropped the crustacean into the pot, where it landed with a big splash, and a hiss.

"*No!*" screamed Chris, running out of the room, his voice so loud it could be heard up and down the street, on both the new and old money sides, until it finally ended with a slam as he shut himself in a closet on the tenth floor.

"That was priceless," Bette observed, still cackling.

Jim just shook his head the way Sam would have. "Woman," he said, "one of these days you're gonna push that biddable-headed boy too far, and when that day comes I'm afeard that something awful boogered up might just happen."

"Oh, pish-posh," Bette chirped. "Stupid people have remarkably thick skins."

But Bette could not have been more wrong. The next morning, when her son stumbled out of the closet and down into the kitchen for breakfast—then out the screen door and off the edge of the porch—it didn't take long for her and Jim to realize that something awful boogered up had indeed happened. Little Chris Elliott was blind.

THREE

Bette took young Chris to all the top specialists in the phone book, most of whom were already all too familiar with the boy's long history of short-lived mental disorders—like his habit of rocking back and forth, his penchant for chewing tobacco, his penchant for chewing fingernails (usually other people's), and of course his penchant for sniffing the leather off the davenport cushions. The doctors threw everything they had at him—partly for the fun of it, but also to see if anything would stick. Just about everything bounced off, except for the jars of Stridex medicated pads, which always made large dents. Elliott eventually concealed the hollows in his forehead with his iconic "Elliott bandanna"—a bold fashion statement that was later ripped off by Stevie Van Zandt, who had been to the same clinic and was trying to conceal some head dents of his own.

Bette never publicly acknowledged her responsibility for Chris's illness, or even that he was sick at all. As she told Louella Parsons, "I simply assumed the boy was going through an awkward stage." The doctors did their best to convince her that Chris was actually suffering from a "conversion disorder," also known as "psychosomatic blindness," or, more archaically, "hysterical blindness," which was an appropriate term because his immature doctors laughed every time he stumbled into their offices and bumped into the examining table.

"Hysterical, my wooden fanny," Bette declared. "I've seen better slapstick at the monkey house. The spaz doesn't even know how to walk into things properly." Then she shoved his head through the drywall. "There, that's how a *real* blind boy would do it."

Despite the doctors' assertion that a psychosomatic illness was *almost* as real as a real illness, and should be treated with *almost* the same level of sympathy—even if you have to pretend a little—Bette refused to see in Chris's so-called affliction anything but another attempt on his part to divert Sam's (or Jim's) attention away from her, and to curry favor with the wealthy elites of the Upper East Side who considered hysterical blindness a true hallmark of aristocracy, like webbed toes, elongated necks, and big badonkadonks.

It didn't help matters either that Chris reveled in his handicap, quickly becoming one of those annoying, godlier-than-thou people who think they're so special just because they're good at pretending to be blind, like Alan Colmes. He started ruining her dinner parties by sitting in the corner with a hat at his feet, playing the harmonica and doing bad covers of Stevie Wonder's "Tears of a Clown."

"What about a lobotomy?" Bette asked Jim one morning over breakfast. "It did wonders for Garbo. She was a royal cock-up until they gave her the old crochet hook."

"No need to go cuttin' on the kid just yet," Jim advised. "The shrinks say he just needs some time to understand what's making him sick."

"Then he's doomed! The boy couldn't understand his way out of a bottomless sack. We might as well ship him off to one of those fancy asylums that pretends to be a boarding school and be done with it."

So in the fall of 1973, Chris was enrolled at the Rudolf Steiner Institute for Gracelessness in upstate New York. It was an expensive boarding school that had little experience with hysterical blindness, but had a lot of experience in pretending to care about the "special" needs of the deformed and/or damaged children of politicians and celebrities. (Kind of like George Bush and Yale.) Bette was drawn to the school's liberal curriculum—the basic tenets of which celebrated a belief in the afterlife, karma, and yoga flying, while dismissing the hygienic properties of mouthwash, deodorant, and underpants. What was more unusual—yet perfect for Chris—was the fact that the school's founder had taken a dim view of the gift of sight. In fact, in 1902, Steiner had penned a significant thesis on the subject, titled *Die Unnoticheit des Anblinks*, or *The Needlessness of Sight*, in which he put forth the notion that "seeing" was just plain "stupid"—or in the more prosaic German, *"Anblinck ist dumm!"* He argued that vision confounded the "higher senses," like the sense of irony or of which wine pairs best with red snapper. But he confessed his true motivations in an offhand remark to his close friend and confidant Wolfgang Goethe, while the two were sunning themselves on the sunny Riviera. "Wolfy," Steiner said, "if we were all to be blind, then we wouldn't have to see the fat people on the beach anymore, yes? Let's make it so." Not long after blinding Goethe, Steiner was committed to the International House for Bedlamites in Dornach, Switzerland, and so never got around to blinding himself as he'd promised. Yet even today, at the school that bears his name, the students are still encouraged to wear blindfolds on all formal occasions.

Although he was glad to be away from San Semolina, Elliott fared poorly at Steiner. He was a teenager by now, and like most teenagers—especially the ones whose birth certificates have the phrase "Your guess is as good as mine" written into the box marked "gender"—Elliott was experiencing chaos and conflict within: the raging hormones of his developing body were dueling with the unclean impulses, filthy thoughts, ultraviolent fantasies, and images of flying cupcakes inside his psychopathic little brain. He couldn't shake the burning desire to burst out, and do something big—but he didn't know what he should be bursting out with, apart from rashes and pimples. He had a vague notion of wanting to be famous like his mother and father, but his fear of failure always held him back. The disastrous Guy Under the Oriental Carpet bit had left him with a debilitating stage fright that he would battle for the rest of his life. This was made worse by the fact that everyone at Steiner knew he had famous parents, so they were always stopping him on the playground to ask him to "do some acting or something," and when he inevitably choked, they would dance around him chanting, "Fraud," or "Hack," or "Poor man's Andy Kaufman."

His grades plummeted, and he became cynical and depressed. He desperately needed some sort of catalyst to help make his dreams come true. Either a catalyst or someone he could just steal ideas from. Already at this early stage, he was beginning to learn that it was better to trust other people's abilities rather than his own, which was really smart because he had none. Fortunately for him, fate was about to lend a guiding hand, in the form of a chance encounter with a student who was every bit as handicapped as he was only subconsciously pretending to be.

It all started when he developed a hopeless crush on Sally Jenkins. She was a sweet, knock-kneed girl with braids like Pippi Longstocking and glasses that made her eyes look like giant frog orbs. She was also covered in tats, always dressed in black, and was fascinated with death—mainly Elliott's. In fact, her first words to him were, "Out of my way or die," and her second words—before shoving him face-first into a locker door when he didn't move fast enough—were, "Better yet, why not both?"

Although he claimed not to be able to see her, he said he was immediately attracted to her distinctive, skunklike musk, "which spoke directly to my loins." He quickly became obsessed with Sally, but sadly it was the kind of *Taxi Driver*–style obsession that had yet to reach the level of popularity it enjoys today. He stalked Sally relentlessly, following her from class to class while voraciously sniffing the air an inch behind her head. He sent her crazy notes begging for a lock of her armpit hair or a piece of her used floss, and he left provocative forget-me-nots on her desk, like globs of corned beef hash or Polaroids of the spongy growths that now covered much of his body.*

For all his efforts, Sally repaid Chris with a Steiner-style restraining order—a straitjacket, concrete shoes, and pants coated with Krazy

---

* *The Elephant Man* had just come out, and the film was so popular with the kids that it had spawned a whole spongy-body-growth craze.

Glue. Resigned that he would never bump uglies with the woman of his dreams, Elliott decided to take his own life, and to do it in full view of everyone as a final display of his undying affection.

During biology class, he dressed himself in a big sandwich board that said, "This is for you, Sally baby," climbed up a ladder, slipped a noose around his neck, and tied the other end to the ceiling fan. A moment later his legs were flailing madly in midair. Unfortunately, the biology lab had high ceilings and everybody was concentrating on their frog guts at the time, so nobody noticed Elliott twirling around up there.

By the time the bell rang, Chris was finally starting to expire. He saw a bright light and felt the presence of relatives who had passed away a long time ago. They struggled to convince him that it wasn't his time yet. "Go back," said his grandmother. "We don't want you here. You're an idiot. And a big phony. You'll just ruin heaven for everybody."

Then two huge hands grabbed his ankles and pulled him down.

When he came to, Elliott was face-to-face with the gigantic Russian exchange student, Adam Milosevic Resnick, the only kid tall enough to have reached him.

"Well, aren't you a strapping fellow," said Chris. Then, remembering that he was blind, he added, "I *hear*."

"*Eto ne tak, kak vy svyazyvaetepetlyu,*" Adam said.*

The two didn't know it then, but it was an auspicious meeting—one that would alter both their destinies, and set them on a course of creative modernism and unmitigated comedic innovation (and also get them in no small amount of trouble).

---

* Roughly, "That's not how you tie a noose."

Their alliance would one day produce such classic works as *Get a Life*, *Cabin Boy*, and an ill-fated Kennedy miniseries on the Reelz network starring Chris as Lance Kennedy—the most brilliant Kennedy brother, but the one the family kept in a closet because he was bald, talked with a lisp, and kept sniffing the leather off the davenport cushions.

During one of his many libel suits, Elliott spoke of the first time he met his best friend and codefendant:

"I had never met anyone who so readily accepted me for who I was and how I smelled without the usual questions about my sanity or whether or not I was dropped on my head as a baby." (Although he failed to add that at the time Adam didn't speak a word of English.)

The rumor at school was that Adam had grown up in a small town in the Kaluga region of the Soviet Union, and when the nuclear power plant there had its big meltdown the radiation gave him giantism—which was why by age fifteen he stood over seven feet tall, and was by all accounts still growing.

But Chris had no way of confirming this rumor, as the language barrier made their communications a bit one-sided at first. Although Adam spoke only Russian, he was able to sign in fluent ASL, but of course Chris couldn't see it (and also didn't know sign language or care to learn. Like most blind people, he looked down on the deaf as inferior beings). But one day at the water fountain they accidentally hit on a working system of communication when Adam splashed some drops on his hand and Chris suddenly called out, "Waaaaah . . . waaaaah . . . whaaaat you're trying to say is that I was going about things all wrong with Sally Jenkins, right?"

Adam nodded his giant forehead furiously.

"Because girls like *bad* boys!" Chris said, slapping his own meager and simian forehead. "I need to be bad . . . bad to the bone! Then and only then will Sally surrender to my intoxicating charms! Adam, you're a genius!"

So the two friends set out to become the worst kids the Steiner school had ever pretended to care about reforming. They started out slow first, getting matching tattoos of actor Ned Beatty, which they stood around showing off in the locker bay in the hopes that Sally would notice.

"Nice tattoos, poseur!" she said, before dropping Chris upside down in a garbage can.

"She noticed!" exclaimed Chris.

Then they began pulling pranks around the school—like greasing the banisters, rearranging the encyclopedias so the volume letters spelled out dirty words, and their favorite—putting slices of American cheese on lightbulbs. By noon, everybody was asking, "Hey, why does it smell so bad in here?" to which Chris replied, "I don't know, maybe somebody burned the cheese instead of cutting it. Did you ever think of that? Eh, Sally? Get it? It's a fart joke. I think."

Sally said, "You guys are so retarded it's hilarious that you can even *breathe*."

"See," he whispered to Adam, "she thinks we're funny!"

Their little pranks continued to escalate, eventually crossing over into the darker realm of pulling wings off flies and smashing snails with a hammer (Elliott had apparently lost his love for all things imbued with life—the love that had caused him to go blind in the first place) until finally they kidnapped Mr. Levine, the math teacher, sealed him in a barrel with a box of Nilla Wafers, buried him alive, and threatened to leave him there until he agreed to give them both

As in gym. He was never heard from again, and in a radio interview twenty years after the fact, Elliott claimed that they had eventually forgotten where they buried the guy. "I still don't know what happened to him," Chris told Scott Muni of WNEW-FM. "He never came back to school, that's for sure. He might still be down there for all I know. Should we organize a search party? Hahahaha."

Sally's reaction was mixed: "I hope you geniuses like shock therapy, because they're going to fry your asses until you drool even more than you already do."

Chris didn't understand this at the time, but she was referring to Steiner's traditional method of "realigning" unruly students with holistic full-body shock therapy. Within moments he and Adam were surrounded by burly nurses with hog-catchers, who quickly dragged them into the special therapeutic chamber between the boiler room and the hydroponic garden.

Chris apparently found the experience too traumatic to discuss, or at least too complicated—he never really understood electricity—because he refused to speak of it to anyone afterward, but fortunately the school's closed-circuit security cameras captured the entire scene.

In it we see the boys shackled and sitting on a long bench at the end of a line of no longer quite so cocky ne'er-do-wells. One by one each is summoned into the back room by Principal Bachmeier and burly Nurse Glockner (think Nurse Ratched meets Lothar of the Hill People), only to emerge an hour later as shadows of their former selves, all their piss and vinegar gone (except for a little on the front of their trousers), replaced by dead eyes, slack jaws, and foamy drool. With looks of total submission on their faces, they shuffled mindlessly out the door and back to class, until only Chris and Adam were left.

"Oh well, I guess you and me are next, huh, Addy old buddy, old friend, old pal of mine," said Chris as he struggled to pull a tin of chewing tobacco out of his pocket. He slipped himself a wad.

"Want some?" he asked, before swallowing, turning green, and puking discreetly behind the bench. "Wait, I forget—it's cigarettes for eating, chewing tobacco for chewing, right? Which reminds me, can I gnaw on your fingernails?"

Adam took the tobacco tin from Chris and then, in a perfect American accent, he said softly, "Thank you."

Despite the security camera's low resolution, you can easily see the dumbfounded expression appear on Chris's face. "Well, look at you! Somebody's been practicing his Englishky." Then he screamed in Adam's ear. "YOU'RE WELCOME, SEÑOR!"

Adam looked down at the tin, which featured a charming caricature of a drunken Indian proudly holding up a bloody scalp while impregnating a white woman behind a casino.

"Mmm," he muttered. "Red Man Plug."

"God damn, Addy!" Chris yelped, stamping his feet like Sammy Davis, Jr. "Keep it up and before you know it you'll be tried-and-true red-white-and-blue!"

"I'm already American, Chris. I'm from Harrisburg, Pennsylvania."

"And that accent is perfect! How long did you have to work on that?"

Adam laughed to himself. "Not any longer than you did on pretending to be blind."

Chris dropped the smile. He suddenly started to twitch. His eyes rolled back in his head. He turned purple, then yellow, then burgundy, and he began shoving wads of tobacco into his mouth until he finally swallowed the entire tin of Red Man, lid and all.

"I have no idea what you're talking about," he said.

"Relax, you don't have to pretend around me. You've got those idiots out there fooled, but us smart guys get it. I mean, I thought I was pulling a good one with the fake Russian thing. But *fake* hysterical blindness? And with the whole 'stupid' act as a cover—it's sheer genius."

"Wait a minute . . ." said Chris, realization finally dawning, "Are you saying you're only *pretending* to be seven feet tall?"

"That's good, never break character. I like it, it's very *meta*. But you've got to be more careful—I saw you when we were watching *F Troop* the other day, and—you were laughing at all the sight gags."

"I was?" said Chris. He looked down at his shackled hands, narrowing his eyes on his wiggling fingers. "Why does this make me think of sausage . . . ?"

Adam continued, "Plus your socks always match, you're the best dart thrower in school, and yesterday you were staring at Sally all through English class going, 'Man she sure looks pretty, doesn't she?'"

A lightbulb suddenly came on over Chris's head. (Steiner was an old school, and the wiring was always a bit jittery.) "Oh!" he cried. "*Conversion* disorder . . . ! That's what the doctors were getting at! I thought they just meant that I was a man trapped in a woman's body."

"Of course those little mistakes could all be part of your act, too, what do I know? There's just so many layers with you. If there was a way to bottle what you do, we could make a fortune."

"I'M CURED!" Chris suddenly stood up so hard that his shackles pulled the bench out of the floor, sending Adam sprawling.

The door swung open and Nurse Glockner's manly voice cried, "Next!"

"Great timing," Chris muttered, suddenly deflated again. "Look at us, Addy, we could have been like Sacco and Vanzetti, Leopold and Loeb . . . Tomlin and Wagner . . . creative partners bound together in a collaborative relationship that might have lasted a lifetime, or at least until I got so high on my own fame that I started hurling whiskey bottles at you from on top of a hotel bed full of cheap whores."

"They have those?" Adam asked.

"But now we're gonna be zapped into a couple of drooling, blithering, blathering, bobbleheaded zombies, like all the rest of these schmoes. So much promise gone to waste. So eleven hundred men went into the water, three hundred and sixteen men come out, the sharks took the rest, June the twenty-ninth, 1945. Anyway, we delivered the bomb." Chris belched. "I really shouldn't have eaten that tobacco tin."

"Boys!" snapped Principal Bachmeier.

"Relax," whispered Adam. "I've got a plan. Just let me do the talking."

The two were led into a dark room (which fortunately also had security cameras) with two metal tables and an electrical generator that looked like a smiling demented robot. They were strapped down, rubbed with a cool mint gel, and fitted with a pair of rubber paddles and a rubber chew toy shaped like a dog bone.

"I'm sorry about this," said the principal. "We try to take a liberal attitude around here, boys being boys and all, but we really do have to draw the line at murdering teachers."

Nurse Glockner added with a sinister laugh, "Don't worry, you boys won't feel anything after the first couple of jolts—ever again."

Adam spit out his chew toy. "Wow, I've really got to hand it to you guys, I never thought you'd take it this far."

The principal looked confusedly down at his clipboard. "Aren't you supposed to be Russian?"

"I mean, you really went all out. . . ." Adam was obviously bluffing, scrambling for what to say next, but he kept so cool that only Chris could tell. "But nobody's watching anymore, you don't have to play along."

"Play along?"

"With our advance promotional campaign of 'fake pranks.' To generate interest for the benefit show we're throwing? Come on, even Mr. Levine was in on it. That's why he let us kidnap him."

"Yeah," said Chris, doing his best to play along, too. "*Let us.* I'm sure he'll tell you all about it as soon as they find him—mwahahaha-hahaha."

"What benefit show?" asked Principal Bachmeier.

"The one to save the school?* Come on, don't tell me you didn't get it."

The principal looked affronted. "Of course I got it! I get things! I'm cool! Nurse Glockner, untie these boys at once!"

And that, as you now know, is the story behind the Steiner school's famous award-winning three-hour performance art version of *The Miracle Worker*. Adam realized that Helen Keller was the perfect role for Chris because it required absolutely no talent. All he had to do was flail around onstage like an idiot, and everyone ate it up. The smart ones assumed he was doing a terrible job on purpose,

---

* I forgot to mention earlier that the Steiner school was in financial trouble, and in constant competition with the much more wealthy Montessori school across the lake, and that if the chairmen didn't come up with $100,000 by Christmas, they would get bought out and turned into a soccer field or a chill-out room or something.

and the plebes just cried a widdle tear every time he managed to say, "W-a-a-a-a-h." Resnick had truly hit on the key to the secret of Elliott's future success, and done so in a manner that went entirely over Chris's head, which meant that from then on, Chris would have no choice but to trust Adam's instincts over his own.

At the time all Chris knew was that he had suddenly become popular. The play not only saved the school,* but instilled in him a bold new confidence. Even Sally Jenkins started to warm up to him—at least, she expressed a reluctant willingness not to enforce the terms of her restraining order. She even agreed to go with him to the Spring Formal. "We'll all be wearing blindfolds, so I guess I can stomach it," she said. "But if you try to kiss me afterwards, I swear I'll cut your fucking lips off."

Everyone wanted to know what was coming next from the new dynamic duo, but when they asked, all Chris would do was wink mysteriously and then pretend to walk into a piece of furniture for another cheap laugh. It was his little way of saying, "I have no idea, but I'm sure Adam will think of something." They were working on their next collaboration, a multimedia extravaganza called *If You Could See What I Can Hear, Then Wait Until Dark and I'll Make Sure the Butterflies Are Free in the Ice Castles*, when, as fate would have it, Bette showed up for parents' weekend, saw what a good time her son was having, spent dinner drinking about a gallon of schnapps and talking about how much more famous she already was at his age, and then the next morning suddenly yanked Chris out of school, fitted him with a tick collar, and sent him off to live with some old relatives in Long Island. "Those tired old broads could use a brilliant, up-and-

---

* Somehow.

coming young entertainer like yourself around the house," she said. "Go liven the place up, you dumb faker."

So Chris and Adam were doomed to postpone their collaboration until years later, when the seeds planted at Steiner would grow into a tree of fame, fortune, sex, love, debauchery, and a few more murders, before being cut down and turned into just another pile of useless show-business bathroom trivia book mulch. But as it turned out, Bette couldn't have done young Chris a better favor.

FOUR

East Hampton—for our more provincial readers—was a small seaside community dotted with picturesque windmills, charming gray-shingled homes, and, for some reason, a museum devoted to the Manson murders. To the east was the great Atlantic Ocean, and to the west the not-so-great Long Island Sound. Between them were sweeping vistas of grassy dunes and miles of buttery soft beaches, while above, huge swarms of murderous black flies roamed the skies, blinding tourists and spiriting unattended children back to their nests in the mod bobs of the filthy rich—which also dotted the community, only with dots made of eighteen-karat gold by Tiffany and Cartier.

The source of this infestation was by far the least mod of the bobs, a gray dilapidated house surrounded by gray concrete walls and overhung by a mysterious, ever-present gray mist that stopped right at the curb. Of course Chris had visited the old beach house several times. As a small child he had spent most holidays there. It would be the perfect retreat for him—a stable environment—a respite from the tensions at home and a place where he could recharge his batteries after all those years at Steiner, where battery-operated devices were strictly *verboten*.

Upon his arrival, he stepped onto the rotting porch and immediately put his foot through a board. Sighing—he was used to this routine—he reached up and knocked on the door.

"That's my head, not the door, baby-boos," said a middle-aged woman in a voice iced with affectation.

"A thousand apologies, Siam," Chris replied. "I guess I'm just so used to pretending to be blind, I didn't see you standing there." He bowed in reverence, like he was addressing Carnac the Magnificent. "I've brought you a present." He held out a carton of melted ice cream.

The woman looked down at the offering with disdain. At fifty-nine, her once beautiful face was now swollen from the ravages of the briny sea air, and her regal forehead was dotted with sunspots and freckles. Alopecia had taken her eyebrows, but her lips—an explosion of amaranth—were still lush and attractive, although tersely puckered at the moment. She was wearing, as she always did, a turban festooned with a single nugget of costume jewelry, and her butt looked like it had been packed by butt-packing professionals into a pair of tight black beachcombers.

"Vanilla," she sneered. "I simply despise vanilla." Then she began to march back and forth while waving a little American flag.

An elderly woman's voice called out from inside the house, "Edie, is someone knocking on the door?"

"No, Mother *dawling*, he was knocking on my head."

"Your head?" cried the voice, as the front door swung open, revealing Big Edie, wheelchair-bound but grinning from ear to ear. "I didn't know your head was made out of wood, dearie. I suppose that's what they mean when they say 'blockhead,' eh, wouldn't you agree, Mr. . . . ?"

Big Edie squinted up at Chris, trying to place him.

Chris said, "It's me, Buddy! Sam and Bette's boy! I'm here to spend the summer with you."

"Oh, Buddy . . ." she said, clearly having no idea who he was. "Edie, our little Buddy has come back to Grey Gardens! Break out the Fancy Feast!"

Though it is well documented that Big Edie and Little Edie Beale were related to Jackie O, it has proven difficult to determine exactly how they were related to Chris. Bette did call them his "cousins," but it's possible that this was just a term of endearment, or—more likely—that Bette just knew that they were crazy enough to take in any stranger who happened to show up on their doorstep claiming to be a relative, or a landscaper, or a bearer of celestial "good news." In fact, there is compelling evidence that Chris's little visits started one holiday road trip when Sam and Bette got tired of him constantly forgetting the words to "One Hundred Bottles of Beer on the Wall," dropped him off on the first porch they could find, and told him to "wing it."

As always, Chris was put up in the Grey Guest Suite, which was between the Grimy Guest Suite and the Suite with No Floor—which used to be known as the Apricot Lounge before Chris started coming to visit. In fact, contrary to popular belief, the Beales were fastidious housekeepers, and Grey Gardens had always been kept immaculate.

When the Maysles brothers first scouted the location for their famous documentary, they weren't happy with it at all. "It just didn't
look like the kind of place where a couple of crazy old women would
live," Albert Maysles told Skippy Lowe. "So we initially canceled the
whole project."

The truth, however, is that Elliott was a disgusting slob. Back
home, Bette ran San Semolina with military precision, never allow-
ing Chris's room to become the slightest bit messy. But at Grey Gardens, he was free to act like he owned the joint—raiding the icebox,
littering the house with garbage, and relieving himself on the potted
plants. Perhaps it was a release of some sort—or a way to mark his
territory, so that the raccoons he let into the house would know who
was boss. One thing is clear, however: once Chris started visiting, it
didn't take long for him to transform the enchanting Grey Gardens
into such a sickening, cluttered hellhole that his cousins gave up on
cleaning it altogether, and eventually on life itself.*

Elliott was closest to Big Edie. She had always sensed potential in
the lad. Perhaps it was because her own show business career had
crashed and burned so early in life, or perhaps it was because she
seemed to think that Chris was Buddy Rich.

"He had an irresistible idiocy about him," she told the Maysles, in
one of the many Chris-related scenes that was cut from the final
documentary. "But oh my, how he could play those drums! Too bad
he was such a pig! I mean look at this place. It wasn't like this until
he showed up, was it, Edie? Edie, tell them it wasn't like this."

---

* When word got out that Chris had transformed the enchanting Grey Gardens
into a sickening, cluttered hellhole, the Maysles brothers returned for another
look and loved what they saw. Filming began immediately.

"Yes, Mother *dawling*. He was a big fat pig. Oink, oink, oink, all the way home." Then Little Edie whispered conspiratorially to the camera, "David, do you realize that if I had been the one to marry Jack Kennedy, *I* would have been the first lady instead of *Buddy*?"*

Chris, in turn, liked to call Big Edie "Sook," because she reminded him of his pet hamster, Beanie, who was also quite the drummer. Sook was both a best friend and a surrogate mother to the boy. Like most crazy people, she simply accepted him for who she thought he was. As Chris would tell Mike Wallace in 1996 (after breaking into his apartment and forcing him at knifepoint to conduct the Q&A), "My favorite season at Grey Gardens was late November. . . . That's when Sook would announce, 'It's fruitcake weather!' Then we'd gather up all the ingredients to make fruitcakes: candied cherries and pineapples, fresh eggs and pecans, sugar and ginger, and a gallon of moonshine liquor from an Indian named Mr. Ha Ha Jones. What fun it was, Mike. Oh, how I wish you and Rooney could have been there. We'd let the fruitcakes cool on the windowsill, and then before anyone could take a bite, we'd sprinkle them with just a smidgen of diphenoxylate to ward off the diarrhea, don'tcha know."

By that point Mr. Wallace was in full cardiac arrest and had lost consciousness. Luckily, when he recovered it turned out that the brief lack of oxygen had erased all memory of the home invasion. Many years later, however, Chris would pen a nostalgic novella called *A Christmas Memory*, recounting the same Grey Gardens fruitcake ritual, but lawyers for Truman Capote's estate would block its publication. *Apparently* Capote had already penned a short story by the

---

* Apparently Little Edie thought Chris (or Buddy?) was Jacqueline Kennedy. Possibly because of his sunglasses—or because she was nuts.

same name, which had a *few* minor similarities—like "fruitcakes," an elderly cousin named "Sook," and an Indian named "Mr. Ha Ha Jones" (which, as Elliott's attorney pointed out, was as common a name as Mr. Ha Ha Smith). Nevertheless, to avoid controversy, Elliott changed the title to *The Christmas Story*, and made it about a boy who wanted a Red Rider BB gun. Again the literary community cried foul, and Elliott was forced to cancel publication. He tried a number of other titles like *The Gift of the Magi*, *The Little Match Girl*, and *The Nutcracker and the Mouse King*, but frivolous lawsuits thwarted him every time. Finally out of frustration he just called it *Fuck Christmas*, which went on to be a bestseller and win him his first Pulitzer Prize.

According to Dr. Adler:

> His obsession with these so-called "fruitcakes" is significant not only because it highlights his devotion to an older woman—a textbook Oedipal manifestation—but also because it is illustrative of a pattern of unconscious absorption (or plagiarism, if you prefer) that would repeat itself throughout his career. He was the great absorber. Never fully confident with his own creations, he became a master of making the work of others appear as if it was his own. This is the sign of a true narcissist—a real *creepola*, a guy who likes to get his ya-yas off but won't extend the same courtesy to his partner. It's shameless chodes like him who could push any woman to the brink of pulling a "Bobbitt," if you know what I mean.

Speaking of pushing women to the brink, June 5, 1974, would turn out to be a momentous day in the life of Chris Elliott. It was a brisk, sunny morning and Big Edie had sent him to the drugstore to pick up some chewing gum, kumquats, and syrup of ipecac. On his way back, he paused to watch some ants consume a detached human ear on the curb. When that fun was over, he caught sight of what he deemed to be the most beautiful, shapely, golden blond white woman he had ever seen.

She was tall, slim, and dripping with sophistication—the kind of babe who makes you think twice about having sexual reassignment surgery. He watched enraptured, his face pressed against the glass of the bakery window as she seductively purchased an apple dumpling from the baker. She was clad in a pair of skintight A. Smile jeans, "wet look" boots, and a skimpy pink boob-tube. Chris knew she would probably be too expensive for him—plus she looked about forty, which struck him as a tad young—but he also knew he somehow had to have her.

She smiled seductively out the window, and then suggestively sank her teeth into her sumptuous little apple dumpling. Chris's face turned red, and he started to sweat. He swallowed hard, and his eyes began to twitch uncontrollably. His pelvis suddenly seemed to have a mind of its own and began thrusting violently back and forth. He managed to flash the woman his best goofy smile, revealing braces clogged with disgusting white gunk. Just then two rubber bands shot out of his mouth, and in his spastic attempt to catch them he dropped the bottle of ipecac, which shattered on the concrete, making him scream, and then he peed his pants.

By now, a crowd had gathered, and someone was asking him if he needed an ambulance. The woman exited the bakery, and when she saw the puddle of cough syrup and urine, she was flattered. But a moment later, a Rolls-Royce pulled up to the curb, and out got a tall skinny blond man in a suit and tie, with Sally Jenkins glasses and a small entourage of artist-looking types.

"Andy!" said the woman. "Look what this charming young man just did."

"It's perfect! You—!" He gestured at three young sycophants who were all dressed exactly like him, but not as well. "I want pictures! Paint five each. The best gets a gold star, the worst gets sent to the Guggenheim."

The three men set up easels and began to paint versions of the now iconic "factory" piece, in which Chris (his head replaced with a particularly stupid-looking soup can) stands forlorn over his mess, the front of his pants wet, and the fumes from the ipecac now making him vomit uncontrollably all over the back of the apple dumpling woman's shoes, as she and Andy Warhol get into his Rolls and drive away.

"Who—" gasped Chris between dry heaves, "was that?"

"Forget her, kid," counseled one of the sycophants. "She's out of your league. She won't even give me the time of day, and I dropped out of Harvard."

Chris's heart sank. The man was right; the encounter had been over before it even began. But though his brain knew it was impossible, the mysterious stirrings in the nether regions of his underpants said otherwise. Something had changed, a crucial step in his sexual development had been achieved. For the first time in his life he longed to be grown-up, an adult, sophisticated—perhaps even *macho*.

He immediately set out trying to make himself into a grown-up man. He started by looking up "man" in the encyclopedia, but the M volume in the Grey Gardens library was full of maggots, so he decided to look in the phone book under "adult store," but everyone he called said he wasn't old enough to shop there. "Well, that's the whole point, isn't it?" he yelled into the phone. "How am I supposed to become an adult if you won't even let me in! What is this, a *Catch-54, Where Are You?*" He was just about to give up when he found a full-page ad in the postiche section of the yellow pages. His eyes lit up. It was too good to be true! He ran straight downtown and within minutes had his face pressed against the glass of Sam Phillips's Sun Studio's Hair Emporium, just under a sign that read: ASK ABOUT OUR NEW SHIPMENT OF ITALIAN FACE MERKINS.

And there, in the back of the store, Chris spied what he deemed to be the most beautiful, perfectly shaped, golden-blond fake beard he had ever seen. Suddenly those mysterious stirrings kicked into overdrive, and he knew he had to have it. Imagine the moment Charlie Chaplin first tried on his famous Hitler mustache, or the moment Hitler first tried on his Charlie Chaplin mustache—it was as if the beard was seducing Elliott, sexily chewing a metaphorical apple dumpling of its very own. "Chris, Chris," it cooed, "buy me, wear me, love me, stick your tongue out through me, and in return, I will make you famous!"

"It's a good fit," Sam Phillips observed, holding up a mirror so Chris could see for himself. "It's you."

It's you. It's you. It's you. The words echoed inside young Elliott's head as he gazed deeply into his reflection, and according to Chris's own remembrance, he began to have visions:

"First, I saw myself as a little boy in Paris. I was being followed by a floating wad of hair with a string attached to it. The wad turned out to be the beard. I noticed the apple dumpling woman floating overhead and grabbed her string, too. I was happy. I felt complete.

Then that vision dissolved, and I was older, cradling a bouquet of Emmy Awards. Then David Letterman (whom I didn't even know yet) handed me the keys to a brand-new Buick LeSabre. 'Thanks for everything, pal,' he said. 'I'd still be tracking downdrafts in Indianapolis if it weren't for you and your beard.' Next I was eating a zeppole at the feast of San Gennaro, when all of a sudden my head was blown off. These images dissolved quickly back to me as a little boy again. I was crying now and missing part of my head—not the important part though, just the part with my brain in it. The strings had slipped from my fingers, and when I looked up, I saw the apple dumpling woman wearing my fake beard. I watched helplessly as she floated up into the sky, disappearing into the vast uncharted expanse of the cold, heatless universe we like to call, um, heaven?"*

"Sir?" Phillips was ready to close up shop.

"Oh. I'm so sorry. How rude of me," Chris said, snapping out of his trance. "Yes, you're quite right, my good man. The beard is simply divine. I must have it. Do tell me how much it would cost a fella?"

"Ten thousand dollars," said Sam.

"Do *wha*?"

All Chris had was the five dollars that the Maysles brothers had paid him for the film rights to the mess he made at Grey Gardens, and that obviously would not be enough. He hung his head low and shuffled out of the store.

He arrived home to find the documentary cameras rolling on

---

* Years later Chris would pen a children's story about a little boy in Paris who befriends a kindly prostitute and a clump of floating hair. The plot didn't resemble a work by any other author, but it was so terrible that the literary community decided to sue just the same.

Little Edie and Sook entertaining visitors in the actual gray garden of Grey Gardens.

Big Edie called out, "Buddy, come and join us. There's some people I'd like you to meet." From the footage you can tell that Chris was in no mood to socialize, but he skulked over nonetheless.

"Here's your stupid ipecac," he said, tossing a few shards of broken glass on the table. "What d'ya want?"

"Buddy, I'd like you to meet my niece, Jacqueline."

Jacqueline Kennedy Onassis extended her hand, as if expecting Chris to kiss it. "Lovely to meet you, Buddy. I understand that we're related . . . somehow."

"Yeah, right. Whatever, sweetheart. Likewise, I'm sure." He shook the tips of her fingers, and turned back to Big Edie. "Is that it? 'Cause I gotta go take a huge dump behind the sofa."

"Wait!" cried Little Edie. "If *she's* Jackie . . ." She looked frantically back and forth between Chris to Jackie. "One of you must be an impostor!"

"Buddy, I also want you to meet a very important person," Big Edie said, grabbing hold of Chris's wrist. "This is Irving Fichman. He's a big-time show business manager, and I've convinced him to take you on as a client."

This was in fact the man who one day would guide Elliott's career to unimaginable heights, but it was difficult to imagine it at the moment. Fichman had to be about ninety years old. His bones creaked as he stood, and just as he began to talk, a huge black fly flew into his mouth. The old man gagged and coughed a disgusting cough that went on for like twenty minutes. Jackie had three cups of tea and a cheeseburger before it was over. Finally, Irving hacked up the fly, which flew directly into Big Edie's mouth. She didn't seem to mind, and simply washed it down with a sip of melted ice cream.

Irving cleared his throat. "Hiya, kid, they tell me your mommy and daddy are famous."

"Aren't you supposed to be dead?" Chris asked.

If you had mentioned the name "Irving Fichman" to anybody else in the business, they would have had the same reaction. He was one of those guys who'd been around forever. "Aren't you supposed to be dead?" was, in fact, his legal middle name.

"I was, kid, I was," sighed Irving. "For about a week, but I'm back now and better than ever."

"What, are you a vampire or something?"

"Yep, just a blood-sucking vampire. That's all I am," he said, and then went into another coughing fit.

Chris glared incredulously at Big Edie. "You gotta be kidding me."

"You know, Buddy, he's really a very lovely man," Jackie injected. "He used to handle my sister, back before it was illegal."

"Honey, do me a favor and keep your trap shut, *comprende*?" Chris snarled back. "This don't concern you, *capiche*?"

"Relax, kid. I've already got a gig lined up for you," Irving proudly announced, producing a thick contract. David Maysles repositioned his camera just in time to catch the change in Chris's expression. Suddenly he was intrigued.

"A gig? What gig?"

"Delivering the *Hampton News*. They'll supply the bicycle. You get fifty cents an hour, plus overtime, and I negotiated the best route for you. Hardly any hills."

"Okay, that's it. I'm out of here." Disgusted, Elliott turned to leave.

"I guess the kid don't want to work," Irving said, shrugging his shoulders.

An off-camera voice interrupted everything. "What a coincidence, I get the *Hampton News* delivered every afternoon."

Elliott stopped in his tracks. There was something about that voice. Was it possible? Could it be? He turned around and there she was, the apple dumpling woman, looking even more dazzling than before.

Jackie introduced her. "Buddy, I'd like you to meet my sister, Lee Radziwill."

"Your sister?" Chris was astonished. "But I thought she was a prosti—"

David Maysles dropped his camera, which was a good thing because according to Fichman, Lee smiled seductively at Chris and took another evocative bite out of her apple dumpling, which made Chris shit his pants, and then he fainted.

Elliott was more than happy to take on the paperboy job now. Not only would he be able to save money for his fake beard, but he also might be able to score with Lee Radziwill. After three weeks he had already saved about nine dollars. It wouldn't be long now before he'd be able to purchase the mock facial hair. Actually, it would be about twenty-five years, but that was nothing to a teenager.

But then the unthinkable happened. One day, while bicycling through the wig district, he was shocked to discover that the beard was no longer on display at the Hair Emporium. It had been sold the day before. "So that's it," he thought. "Some other lucky stiff is probably wearing it right now, getting fed bits of apple dumpling through its feathery golden down. . . ." He was so enraged that he chucked the *Hampton News* right through the window. This made him feel manly, so he touched his face to see if maybe he'd suddenly grown a beard of his own—but he hadn't. Besides even if he *could* produce actual facial hair, the rats at Grey Gardens would just nibble it off while he was sleeping. So he threw another paper—this time into the window of the apple dumpling shop. That felt good, too, so he kept on in this fashion, leaving a trail of destruction along his designated route.

It was dusk by the time he reached Lee Radziwill's house, but he hadn't cooled off yet. He let her paper fly, but it landed short on her front lawn. Lee came out in a skimpy see-through negligee, and Chris craned his neck to watch her ass as she bent over to pick it up. . . .

BAM!

He was suddenly splayed out over the hood of a parked car. He raised his head just long enough to hear some tweety birds (which had been imported from South America to help reduce the fly population), and then fell back, unconscious.*

When he came to, Elliott was lying on the sofa in Lee's house. She was in another room, but years later he told friends that he could see her shadow on the wall. He watched it closely. It appeared as though Lee was preparing for some sort of elaborate sex romp, placing a variety of provocative items on a tray like handcuffs, vibrators, a saddle, and a portable generator—but when she appeared, there was only a pot and two cups on the tray that she held.

"Coffee?" she asked, handing Chris a full cup.

---

* This was the scene that years later would appear in the opening credit sequence of Elliott's iconic television show, *Get a Life*. Lee Radziwill—fresh from bombing on Broadway in a horrendous revival of *The Philadelphia Story*—was more than happy to re-create her role as the horny housewife with the sumptuous ass.

"Oh. Yes, please," Chris responded. "I love coffee. Ow, ow, ow, ow, ow!" He burned his lips on it. "Damn, woman, that be some hot java!"

"So what do you like to do on the island, Buddy?" Lee asked.

Chris was nervous. "Oh, I like basketball, but baseball's good, too. At least with baseball, you don't get 'round shoulder' from dribbling."

"Right," said Lee.

"I also like to sing, although for a change, you can always whistle . . . or fart!" He laughed so hard that he actually *did* fart, and then he threw up.

"Ah-huh." Lee wasn't exactly sure how to handle this guy (maybe with rubber gloves?).

"Tide's coming in," Chris observed. "In more ways than one, right? It's high tide in my pants is what I mean."

"Why don't we be quiet for a little while?" Lee suggested politely.

"Oh, sure. Quiet is good, although I'm also partial to base-ball, but—"

"Shhh." Lee pressed her finger to his lips. Then she moved to the record player and put on some mellow music. They began to dance, but Chris hung on her like dead weight, and after a moment she collapsed under his girth.

"I have a better idea," she said, standing up and straightening her hair. She guided Elliott into the bedroom and instructed him to "just put the money on the dresser."

"Money? Wait a second, so you *are* what I thought you were? Jeez, whatdya know about that? Small world, huh? Well, sorry, but I don't have anything smaller than this." And he dumped out a handful of seashells on her dresser. "You can give me the change in the morning."

Lee smoothed the bedspread with the palm of her hand. "Come here, boy. You've managed to charm me with your moronic ways."

Suddenly Elliott became even more nervous. "Um, I . . . I'm ah . . . I'm not sure I know exactly how . . . to . . . um . . . I mean . . . I'm sure with a little guidance or if you have an instructional manual, I might be able to . . . you know . . ."

"Maybe this will help." Lee reached under the pillow and pulled something out—something as golden and beautiful as she.

"The beard! That's my beard." Chris was ecstatic. "How did you get it?"

"Well, I knew you had your eye on it. . . ." She held it up in front of him, dangling it like a toreador's cape. "And I thought you might need a little boost. . . ."

Chris felt a sudden rush of confidence. He crawled toward the beard, stomping one foot on the bedspread like a bull's hoof. "You're in for a rare treat now, sugar!" Then he dropped trou and charged straight for the beard, but Lee pulled it away at the last moment, causing him to crash headfirst into the wall.

"You've got to catch me first," Lee said behind him, as Chris pried his head free. Then he turned to see her sitting naked on the bed with nothing but a pillow on her lap—and *his* beard on *her* face.

"Rawr!" she growled in a suddenly deep and manly voice. "Come and give your Papa Bear a big ol' kiss."

"Uh . . ." Chris felt the mysterious feelings in his loins suddenly shrivel up. "Maybe we can just hold each other and talk."

Lee began to swagger toward him like a longshoreman, twitching her now moist and hairy lips. "Whattsamatta, kid, you scared? Don't worry, I won't make fun of that little monkey double dick of yours, although I gotta say I've never seen anything like it. It looks like a two-headed turtle! When you croak, you should donate that thing to the Phallological Museum. They'd make a fortune on a beaut like that. Now come here, honey, Papa Bear knows how to treat you right. Smoochy-smoochy!"

She bent down to press her hairy lips to his mouth, and Chris—with his pants still around his ankles—screamed, then hopped across the bed and out the window, landing on a pile of garden hoes in the backyard. He got on his bike and pedaled away as fast as he could. This time he didn't even bother returning to the Beales'. He just rode straight to East Hampton Harbor, jumped into the water, and swam toward the lights of the nearest ship—which turned out to be a Carnival Cruise liner bound for Hawaii. When he was discovered a day later, he was forced to work as a cabin boy to pay for his passage (sound familiar?). His boss was a young entertainment director named Kathie Lee Gifford, who recruited him for her stage show but unfortunately kept making awkward passes at him—like tricking him into getting so drunk that he would hit on her so egregiously that she had to beat him bloody with a shuffleboard paddle. Needless to say, she never got very far with the kid, especially because on their third day out of port, while Chris was rehearsing his new "Guy Under the *Seas*" character, he somehow accidentally opened the wrong hatch and flooded the forward hold. The ship sank immediately, and all hands—especially Chris's hands—were lost at sea.*

---

* Elliott had been lost at sea for only about two days when Bette donated his clothes to charity, rented out his bedroom to a homeless man, and adopted a daughter, named B. D. Hyman, to take his place. (And we all know how that turned out.)

FIVE

By the time he washed up onshore, Chris's body was an oozing collage of ulcers, saltwater blisters, and festering fish bites. For weeks he had drifted along the equatorial current, clinging to Kathie Lee's inflatable "dream hubby," his only companions a pool of oil named "Slicky," the occasional floating corpse-in-a-cooler, and of course those pesky Dorados. . . .

Known for being aggressive, the Dorado, or "Horn-Dog" fish, can range in length from two to six feet, and are distinguishable by their vibrantly colored torsos. Their flanks and bellies are adorned by long blue dorsal fins that extend from their blunt noses all the way down to their concave anal fins, which are unusually large and—let's go ahead and say it—*sexy*. The females boast juicy, red lips and long black eyelashes (which they bat coquettishly when in heat), and their large, sumptuous breasts appear astonishingly human (especially if you've been drinking seawater for close to twenty-five days). After the humiliating experiences with Sally Jenkins and Lee Radziwill, not to mention enduring Kathie Lee's nauseous advances, Chris had sworn off women for good, but this didn't stop him from "bonding" with one of these especially assertive Dorados.

He named her Marsha Mason, because she looked like the famous actress—especially when she would wag her pelvic fin at him disparagingly, like she was maybe scolding Richard Dreyfuss. In the beginning, she would appear only once a day, circling him a few times with an air of detachment, then swimming away. Gradually, however, she came around more often, and it wasn't long before the two were up all night sharing secrets and arguing politics. In fact, you may have heard that in 1980 the *National Enquirer* reported that Chris Elliott lost his virginity to "actress Marsha Mason." Like most *Enquirer* articles, there was a germ of truth in it, but as usual they'd missed the bigger picture. Chris's Marsha Mason had never acted a day in her life.

But at least the deed had finally been done. Elliott's pipes had been officially cleaned—sort of—and for the first time in his life he felt like a man, albeit Aqua-Man. Unfortunately, a week later, the fickle Dorado left him for a great white shark that was hung like a bull . . . uh, shark.

Heartbroken, Elliott strangled Marsha Mason and ate her carcass. It was the first time he'd ever strangled and cannibalized a girlfriend, but it wouldn't be the last. Afterward, he felt terrible about it and resolved to kill himself by jumping off the edge of the ocean, which of course was impossible, but, come on, folks, give him a break! The guy was out of his fucking gourd by then! He'd been floating around without food or fresh water for like a fucking month. You try it!

Luckily, before he could do any real damage to himself, the currents landed him on the soft sands of a remote tropical island. The experience that followed can be seen as a testament to his unwavering will to survive. All his life, whether battling failure, insecurity, addiction, endless lawsuits, murder raps, sexual abnormalities, or the trials of being a black man in America, Elliott managed to maintain a steadfast and resolute strength. He was, after all, a true survivor.

He struggled to stand, hampered by the rotting carapace that he once lovingly referred to as his "skin," but which now hung like hot dripping paraffin from his brittle chicken bones. Looking out to sea, he narrowed his bloodshot eyes and scanned the horizon for any sign of life, but unfortunately all he could see were the coast guard boats that were looking for him, which he naturally mistook for pigeons.

His situation was dire and he knew it. Still, he must have felt a slight sense of relief, not only because he was on dry land, but also because he was far away from the failures that had dogged him back in the "civilized" world. Perhaps he could start life all over again on this remote island, he thought, and so immediately set about making the place feel like home—or what he imagined "home" to be.

He gathered some sand, mud, tree sap, and water to make a campfire. For hours he rubbed the ingredients between his thighs just as he was taught in Boy Scout training—but unfortunately his thighs were too damp to catch fire (a chronic problem he would endure his entire life).

Next, he tried writing a message in the sand:

Hello everyone up there in that big, beautiful marvel of German in-
genuity we call an airplane. What's the movie today? Don't you hate
it when the guy next to you hogs the armrest? Well, here's why I'm
writing. See, I have a little problem. . . .

But the tide came in and washed away the whole stupid message
before he could even get to the part about being marooned on an
island.

He was hungry now, so he searched the beach for something edible, but all he could find was a watertight box of MREs that had
washed ashore. Having heard rumors about how awful army food
was, he couldn't bring himself to try them. Then a horrifying thought
crossed his mind: *If I don't find something to eat soon, I may have to eat
myself just to survive. . . .*

At that moment, he spied a lone coconut lying on the sand. His
prayers had been answered! With both hands, he lifted the heaviest
rock he could find and brought it down hard. He hammered away at
the thing, trying desperately to smash open its stubborn shell, but its
casing was even harder than the rock, and he couldn't dent it. Each
time he tried, the rock tore deep into his flesh, and his hands began
to bleed profusely.

"Why me, Lord?" he cried. The isolation and loneliness were
finally beginning to overwhelm him. "What have I ever done to
you, except filch a few measly bills out of that stupid offering bas-
ket at St. John's, where the priest made me keep my fingernails
extra long?"

He plopped back down in the sand, broken and defeated. Grabbing hold of the coconut, he was about to chuck it into the surf, but found that he was too weak to even lift it.

Years later, he recounted the experience that followed to his friend Tom Hanks, who was researching a role for some new feel-good family movie or something:

"I stared at that coconut for like three days, Tom. On the third day, I noticed my bloody handprint made it look like it had a face. I was so desperate for any kind of interaction—human or fish or otherwise—that I took my finger and refined the features with more blood. Then I started talking to the thing—like it was my friend or something. Call me crazy, Tom, but I actually named it Cokey. You believe that shit?"

Hanks yawned. "That's totally implausible," he said snottily, and then started frantically texting Robert Zemeckis.

"Yeah, okay, whatever, pal," Chris replied, equally snottily. "Why don't you go eat yourself a box of chocolates, asshole—'cause that's what 'life's like,' right? Blow me."

The two never spoke again.

Back on the island, with tears streaming down his face, Chris began to confess his innermost feelings to his new friend, Cokey the coconut. "Cokey. I've failed at everything I've ever tried. I'm just a big loser—a phony! That's all I am. Plus I have a forked penis, and I only screw fish. What's the use in going on? Oh, Cokey, say something, will ya? Talk to me, you big old crazy coconut."

You can imagine how surprised he was when it actually *did* start talking back to him.

"Owchy magowchy," it mumbled. "You really did a number on me."

"Oh, um . . . sorry about that?"

"Yeah, sure you are. Look, fella, you gotta stop feeling sorry for yourself. We all mess up from time to time—that's part of life. Show business is ninety percent perception, five percent tenacity, fifty percent luck, and ten percent math. Talent's got nothing to do with it. In fact, talent just gets in the way—so you're actually ahead of the game in that department. Also your forked penis must come in handy when you're out of chopsticks."

The coconut laughed heartily at that, and so did Chris, even though he had no idea what it meant.

After an awkward pause, the coconut continued, "Listen, if you can get me out of this predicament, I'll teach you everything I know about acting—*and* everything I know about women. I've balled the best of 'em—including Stella Adler backstage at the Harold Clurman, during the second act of *Truckline Cafe*, so don't talk to me about sex, you fucking insect, 'cause I've been around the block a few times."

Chris was confused. He had left reality somewhere far behind. Was this coconut really talking to him? And did it really just call him an "insect"? And what was this "predicament" that it was referring to?

He crawled around to the other side of the coconut, and there, to his surprise, was *another* face—only this one wasn't drawn in blood. It was a *real* face, dripping with blood. He recognized it immediately. How could he not? The features were unmistakable.

"Marlon Brando!" Chris exclaimed.

The actor was buried up to his neck in the sand.

"Oh, you recognize me, wonderful," Marlon muttered. "How 'bout being a mensch and getting me out of here?"

"Recognize you? Of course I recognize you. Me and my friend Adam are like, your biggest fans!" Chris broke into an impersonation. "I'm-ah, going to-ah, make you an offer you can't-ah refuse-ah?"

"That's a great Chico Marx," said Brando. "He was a real cocksman, you know? They all were, although Harpo was half a fag. Now how 'bout digging me out of here?"

"How'd you get down there, anyway?" Chris asked as he scooped the sand away from Brando's chins.

"My natives," he grumbled. "I guess I pissed them off. I was performing my one-man version of *Last Tango in Paris*, as usual, but for some reason they did not cotton to it. They behaved themselves until the middle of Act Seven, when I slipped on the butter and fell on my ass. Then they rushed the stage and buried me up to my neck as punishment."

"It sounds like you kind of deserved it," Elliott said.

Brando huffed. "Everyone's a critic."

Within a few days, Elliott had managed to dig enough of the sand away to free the actor's massive neck and shoulders, after which he crawled out of his hole and stood majestically before an awed Chris, who felt compelled to kneel. (Mainly because Brando immediately started pushing on his head while yelling, "Kneel, simpleton!")

The actor was wearing a traditional Hawaiian-print muumuu, which was covered in wet sand and hermit crabs. His bald noggin was caked with dried blood, and he looked to weigh about four hundred pounds.

"Welcome to Tetiaroa!" he exclaimed. "You are now flesh of my flesh, blood of my blood, and shit of my shit. I shall call you 'Hinatea,' which means 'white granddaughter.' Does this please you?"

"Um, yeah, sure . . . I guess."

"Good. Now rise, granddaughter, and come with me. There is much you must learn, plus I'm fucking starving."

As fate would have it, Chris had washed up on the shores of Brando's private island, called Tetiaroa, meaning "actor who's so fucking fat he has to stand with his legs apart." Tetiaroa was just one of a number of small islands that were part of an atoll located about forty miles north of Tahiti. Marlon discovered it while he was shooting *Mutiny on the Bounty* back in 1960, and was so taken with its lush vegetation, yellow sands, and easy native women, that he had to have it. It was an escape for him—a paradise—a raw utopia, and the antithesis of the Hollywood life that the actor detested. Yet for all its natural beauty, Brando had done his share of development on the island, and he ran the place less like utopia and more like Jonestown.*

"Tasteful!" Chris observed, admiring the lobby of the Tetiaroa Hotel, a huge simulated thatched-roof hut that looked like an even more grotesque version of the Tiki Room at Disneyland.

A beautiful, dark-skinned woman wrapped in a skimpy sarong and sporting a blue jacaranda flower in her hair approached them.

"Yo-rah-nah! Yo-rah-nah!" she pronounced excitedly, which means "Welcome back." Then she pressed her body against Marlon's and said, "Where you been, Poe-Poe? We be so afeard. Where you been?"

---

* This may explain why the indigenous population was negatively predisposed to the lame theatrical productions Brando compelled them to endure every Saturday night.

"It doesn't matter where I been. Bow your head to Hinatea," Brando said, introducing Chris with a flourish. "He saved Poe-Poe's life. Now he belong to Poe-Poe. Poe-Poe gonna make him his butt boy."

"What fun!" Chris exclaimed enthusiastically. "I've been meaning to take up smoking."

The woman moved in close to Chris. "Ma-roo-roo. Ma-roo-roo," she purred, bowing her head respectfully. "That mean 'Thank you' in your language." Then she kissed Chris on the lips (plus her tongue accidentally slipped down his throat—about three times). "And that mean 'I'm fine! Thanks for asking.'"

To say that there was electricity would be an understatement. It's more accurate to say that there was an all-out volcanic eruption down on Main Street in Elliott's loin town.

"Granddaughter," Brando said to Chris, "may I be so bold as to introduce Tarita, the island virgin."

"The pleasure is all mine," Elliott cooed. He was flushed, and he was trying to hide a boner, which was hard to do without skin, but Brando must have seen it because he smiled slyly and winked at Chris. Then Marlon turned to Tarita and said something in Polynesian. He gestured back and forth between her and Chris, and Tarita replied, "Ee-yo-ee. Ee-yo-ee," which means "And how!"

"Jakunta will show you to your room." Marlon clapped his hands three times, and a native in a bellhop uniform appeared. "After you freshen up," Brando continued, "the natives will throw you a real tah-mah-rah."

"A what?"

"A Tahitian luau in your honor!" Then Marlon whispered into Chris's ear, "Afterwards, maybe you and Tarita can go somewhere private and 'peel the old pineapple,' if you get my drift?" and then he made a lewd gesture and giggled lasciviously.

As Chris was led away, he glanced behind him. He was fairly sure afterward that Tarita had winked at him, and then flashed her bush.

*   *   *

The "tah-mah-rah" wasn't anything like what Captain Cook first witnessed in Tahiti in the 1700s. It was more like a lame theme party from the 1950s. The outdoor area was decorated with cheap tiki torches, cardboard cutouts, and Styrofoam totem poles. The "natives," clad in fake grass skirts and plastic leis, stood around bored. A few of them were halfheartedly doing the limbo under a stick that was at least five feet off the ground. Another group took weak swings at a piñata shaped like a sombrero. The haunting strains of Don Ho's "Tiny Bubbles" emanated out of a record player manned by Jakunta, who was desperately toking a bong, and a fully cooked spiral ham hung on a spit over the fire. Everybody sat around in a circle drinking Hawaiian Punch out of paper cups that said "Luau" on them—just in case anybody had forgotten what they were doing.

Brando was the only one having a good time. He sat cross-legged like a chief, pointing at various bare-chested female natives and giggling like an immature kid. When he saw Chris, he gestured for him to join the festivities. Elliott sat down next to him. Tarita was sitting on the other side. And when they locked eyes, Chris winked at her, and she licked her lips seductively, and then flashed her bush again.

Brando laughed. "Later, you two. Later." Then he offered Elliott a bowl of what looked like brown sludge. "I won't take no for an answer," Marlon said. "Jakunta makes it special for me every day. He calls it 'Jakunta's poi.'" Jakunta suppressed a laugh, as Elliott tasted a finger full of the gunk. Right away, he knew it definitely was *not* poi—at least not in the traditional sense of the word, but he was literally starving, so he gulped it down.

"Interesting," he observed politely. "It has an unusual undertaste."

Brando laughed. "Yeah, like shit!" Then he got up and clapped his hands again. A bunch of fat, shirtless native men joined him in the center of the circle. They each produced a bunch of bananas and threw them down at their feet. Jakunta placed Brent Fabric's inimitable "Alley Cat" on the turntable, and a wonderful, ancient ceremony commenced.

Brando and the fat natives danced around the clumps of bananas. Their moves seemed utterly tribal, yet they had a jazzy, boogie-woogie swing to them as well. There was a bit of Caribbean influence, too, mixed in with some flamboyant ass thrusts, à la Bob Fosse. Chris felt like he was witnessing something that no other civilized man had ever seen. He was mesmerized.

After a while, Marlon grabbed Elliott's hand and pulled him up. At first Chris was shy, but with some prodding from Marlon he eventually joined in. "Just let yourself go!" Brando shouted. "Feel the beat! Let your fingers do the walking!" and before he knew what was happening, Elliott was blissfully dancing around the piles of bananas.

"Shuffle your feet!" Brando instructed. "Now shake your hand. Bounce your head back and forth. Now smile like a moron!" Chris was hooked. It was the most amazing out-of-body experience he'd ever had. With Brando's encouragement, he felt all his inhibitions falling away—all those hang-ups that had kept him from being who he *really* was. Chris began to feel light-headed, and also really horny. Tarita was watching him dance, and Chris was watching her watch him—and Brando was watching the both of them watching each other. The pulsating rhythm of "Alley Cat," the heat, the sweat, the flames—it was all so intoxicating. When the Banana Dance reached its fever pitch, everyone seemed to be in a trance, and the juices inside Elliott were ignited. Brando nodded to him and Chris knew what he meant. He left the circle, took hold of Tarita's hand, and the two stole away into the night, as Brando watched them with a look of fatherly approval on his face.

The couple ran through the moonlit forest, but gradually Chris fell behind and lost his way.

"Tarita!" he called out. "Tarita?"

Just then a Nacunda Nighthawk sounded off right by his ear, and a Komodo dragon hissed and bit his ankle. He screamed and ran deeper into the rain forest. Suddenly he was grabbed from behind.

"Watch out!" Tarita warned, and Chris looked down just in time to see that he was about to run off the edge of a cliff. Had it not been for her, he would have plunged about sixty feet or so into the crashing surf below.

"It called 'Dead Man's Bluff,'" Tarita explained. "Not very original, I know, but Brando name everything and nothing we can do about it. Bad spirit live here. You never come back here again. Too dangerous. Come now, you follow me. Much to do." She giggled and ran back into the jungle, and Chris ran after her.

They ended up at a ramshackle building that had an old sign

outside that read DOLE PINEAPPLE FACTORY. Once inside, Elliott wasted no time. He took hold of Tarita, and without a word, he ripped off her sarong and threw her on top of a pile of pineapples, where he proceeded to demonstrate everything the Dorado had taught him.

Tarita would be scarred for life.

*　*　*

Brando was as good as his word. Over the next year he schooled Elliott in the arts of acting *and* in making love (although by this point Chris didn't need much help in that department anymore).

In terms of acting, Brando taught Chris the Sandy Meisner technique, the Strasberg method, and the Wally Cox approach, and in terms of sex, he taught him the Ron Jeremy style, the Johnny Holmes method, and the Harpo Marx system. They worked from dawn to dusk. Later in life, Chris Elliott would credit his uninhibited exhibitionism to the encouragement and guidance of his mentor. If it wasn't for Marlon, who knows if Chris would ever have taken his shirt off on national television, and if he hadn't, who knows how the world would be different today. We all might be goose-stepping down Fifth Avenue right now.

To test Chris's skills, Brando decided that the two of them would put on an all-male version of *A Streetcar Named Desire* for the natives. Chris recalls the rehearsal period being a "grand and magical" time in his life. "After rehearsing all day with the great Marlon Brando, I would take the beautiful Tarita to the Pineapple Factory and make my own particular brand of sweet love to her."

However, opening night proved catastrophic, and a wedge was driven between master and apprentice that would persist for the rest of their lives. (In fact, the wedge would become so big that by the time Chris achieved stardom, Brando would deny even having known him.)

It was August 6, 1979, and the natives were restless—mainly because the benches in the little thatch-roofed theater were incredibly uncomfortable. Act One went off without a hitch, but just before the curtain went up on Act Two, Chris noticed Jakunta backstage whispering something to Marlon. Whatever it was, it infuriated Brando so much that he picked up the pygmy stage manager and threw him into the orchestra pit.

It was during the pivotal Scene Ten that things turned really weird. This of course is the scene where Stanley Kowalski has his way with Blanche DuBois.

The scene opened with Chris playing Blanche, decked out in a crumpled evening gown and heels, sitting before a makeup mirror, adjusting a jeweled tiara.

Brando enters as Stanley.

MARLON: Oh, hi, Blanche.
CHRIS: (speaking in a falsetto with a horrible southern accent) How's my sister?
MARLON: Oh, she's fine. Come to think of it, maybe you wouldn't be so bad to interfere with.

(Chris was startled. That line wasn't supposed to come for a while. Brando had jumped about four pages of dialogue. Elliott tried to get them back on track.)
CHRIS: Um . . . and how's the baby?

MARLON: Oh, you want some roughhouse? Okay, I'll give you some roughhouse. (Brando picked up Chris and carried him toward the bedroom set, while Chris pounded his chest.)

CHRIS: No, wait, you're skipping lines!

MARLON: We've had this date with each other from the beginning, fucko!

CHRIS: Fucko? That's not in the script! Help! Somebody help me! He's out of his mind!

At this point in the actual play, the lights would have faded out and whatever happens between Stanley and Blanche in the bedroom would have been left to the imagination. However, the rage that had possessed Brando took over, and not only did the lights stay on, absolutely *nothing* was left to anyone's imagination, least of all Chris's.

This was worse than *Last Tango*. Disgusted, the audience rushed the stage ready to haul both actors out to the beach, but Brando held them back.

"Wait!" he cried. "This outsider has defiled my wife."

Chris said, "Your wife?"

"The island virgin?" a native asked, and the rest of the mob murmured to one another, "Island virgin . . . island virgin . . . defiled . . . no talent bastard actor with no chin, poor man's Andy Kaufman," etc.

Brando went on. "He has stolen her innocence and now nothing but ill fortune will plague our island paradise!"

"Hold on a second!" Chris protested, getting up from the bed and straightening his slip. "You *wanted* me to have her! The night of the luau you were *encouraging* me to take her somewhere and sex her up! I know you were!"

"What are you talking about?" Brando argued. "I was *encouraging* you to go peel some pineapples. That's how we make our money here. We peel pineapples for the good folks at Dole. We all have to do our share."

"Huh?" Chris was totally confused. "No . . . no—that's not right. You wanted me to have down and dirty sex with her! You even made that gross gesture with your hands!"

"Idiot!" Brando said, and he did the gesture again. "Peeling pineapples. Get it?"

Chris was speechless (for once).

Jakunta proclaimed, "The outsider must die!" A drumbeat started, and the natives began to chant something threatening in Polynesian. A tear rolled down Marlon's cheek as he lamented, "You've ruined everything. Tarita is defiled, and the wrath of Tefaton is upon us." A thunderclap sounded just as Brando lifted a big machete high over his head, prompting Chris to scream and run like hell.

The rest of the natives pulled out machetes, and they all gave chase.

Elliott ran through the jungle. Thorns and branches cut his legs and arms as he went. He fell like ten times before he realized he was still in heels. Discarding the shoes, he ran as fast as he could. He ran until he came to a clearing, and then luckily he stopped short, because otherwise—yet again—he would have run straight off the edge of Dead Man's Bluff. He was trapped. There was no way out. Brando and the natives were hot on his trail. He had only two choices: face the angry mob or jump.

His Boy Scout training kicked in again, and he quickly fashioned a small life preserver out of a few coconuts and some torn strips from his evening gown. He watched the waves closely, counting, trying to gauge the perfect moment to throw it in. His Steiner education had left him sadly lacking in the math department—especially after he murdered his math teacher—so it was really just by sheer luck that after he threw the preserver off the cliff the waves pulled it away from shore. Now it was Chris's turn. He readied himself to jump, counting, "One . . ." But just then Brando emerged from the bushes, brandishing his machete and screaming like a banshee.

"Two-three!" and Chris quickly jumped. Brando watched Chris fly off the cliff. Down, down, down he tumbled until he hit the waves below with a sickening thud. This time he had miscalculated and landed in only about a foot of water. He broke both legs and his coccyx, but managed to grab hold of the life preserver, and the strong currents quickly whisked him out to sea.

By now, Jakunta, Tarita, and the natives had joined Marlon on Dead Man's Bluff, and they all watched as Elliott floated beyond the reef and out into open ocean. A moment later they observed him being plucked from the water by a bunch of paparazzi in one of the many boats that regularly buzzed Marlon's island.

"I swear on the hernias of my mother," Brando said, "that even if it takes me the rest of my life, I'm going to find that boy—and when I do, I'm gonna kill him—and then if I'm hungry, I'm gonna eat him."

Tarita sighed. "Ee-la-mono," she said wistfully, which roughly meant "Good-bye, my sweet weirdo with the forked penis, who took advantage of me on some pineapples . . . but understandably, I guess, given the language barrier . . . I wish him the best, may he go on to fame and fortune, or at least some reasonable facsimile thereof."

Within a week, Elliott would be back Stateside—and with the nightmare of Tetiaroa buried deep in his subconscious, he was finally ready to begin his career in earnest.

SIX

U p to this point, Elliott had led a life of reckless abandon, indecision, and false starts. He was chasing vague dreams with little or no discipline, and striking out in all directions without any clear focus or determination. Yet after he escaped Brando's island, he was filled with a renewed sense of ambition and confidence, mainly because he now had a traumatic past to suppress, as hard as he could, preferably by numerous manic and desperate attempts to acquire love and attention.

Opting not to return to San Semolina, he rented a small flat in Greenwich Village and refused financial aid from his parents, which was a prudent decision considering none had been offered. His days were spent pounding the pavement for a survival job, while his nights were spent at the White Horse Tavern drinking root beer schnapps and debating politics with the likes of young Jon Stewart, young Bill Maher, old Jack Reed, and old Louise Bryant. Surprisingly Elliott, who had the IQ of an Earth shoe, was able to hold his own with this group of highly intellectual activists. As Bill Maher remembers it, "He made some interesting points. Once, when I was complaining about Republicans who say they don't 'deify' their candidates the way Democrats do—ahem, *Ronald Reagan?*—I turned to Elliott and asked his opinion. He thought about it for a minute and then said, 'I believe deification is best practiced in our nation's rest stops.' Now I'm certain he didn't understand the irony in his statement, because obviously the guy was missing some gray matter, but by equating 'deification' with 'defecation,' he had made a rather brilliant observation—albeit in a Chauncey Gardiner kind of way. Still, I don't think Mark Twain—who was the *original* Chauncey Gardiner—could have said it any better."

In the fall of 1980, Elliott ran into an old friend from a prenatal acting class named Bernie Berkley. Berkley had just started up an improv troupe called The Five and Dime, and they had been performing at various dinner theaters, bathhouses, and empty carports all around town. Improv was all the rage at the time. Like the skiffle bands of the early sixties, groups of rebellious teens, influenced by the seditious satire of Monty Python, Firesign Theatre, *Saturday Night Live*, and Ronald Reagan, formed improv troupes—with inimitable names like The Groundlings, The Committee, The High Heeled Women, The Farce Side, Hams on Rye, Jabba the Nuts, Lord Have Myrrh, See?, Hold the Ketchup, Pass the Mayo, The Rib Ticklers and Jamie, The Toasted Bialis with a Schmeer, Mother May I, Lather Rinse and Repeat, Helter Schmelter, The Capturing the Friedmans, The Chortle Queens, Fascist Bunions, Peeps A-Poppin', and of course

The Ramalama Ding Dongs—and they honed their acts wherever they could find an audience. Back then every street corner was alive with the sounds of young thespians improvising bits of social commentary, usually veiled in campy send-ups of *The Exorcist*, *Lassie*, or *The Wizard of Oz*. There was a palpable electricity in the streets. Unfortunately not all the kinks had been worked out of the new palpably electric streets, so many ambitious young comics were accidentally electrocuted. But those who survived went on to give rise to a defiant new style of comedy. This "New Wave," led by edgy talents like J. J. Walker, Gary Mule Deer, and David Letterman (the three founding members of The High Heeled Women), would change the face of comedy forever, and ultimately redefine our collective sense of humor. Elliott wanted to be part of this exciting new movement, and so he eagerly joined The Five and Dime—so eagerly, in fact, that he didn't even wait for Bernie to ask. He just kept showing up at rehearsals with coffee and scones, and no one could figure out how to get rid of him.

One of their first bookings was at the Ravenite Social Club down on Mulberry Street. It wasn't a dinner theater, per se. In fact, it wasn't a theater at all. It was just a storefront that had been converted into an informal bar with the addition of a few tables and some folding chairs. It was frequented by a bunch of old Italian guys, which Chris thought was great, "because," as he recalled, "*young* Italian guys might have had the energy to actually get up and leave, right?" He had no idea at the time that it was actually the infamous hangout of the powerful Gambino crime family, or that the proprietor was Neil "The Tall Man" Dellacroce himself. He'd just assumed it was a retirement home for pasta aficionados.

Though he should have realized something was off when at the start of the show he called out for the audience to suggest an occupation and somebody yelled back, *"Undertaker!"*

"Okay," Chris said. "Undertaker, that's a fun one. I guess you old folks do do a lot of dying, don'tcha? Now, how 'bout a place?"

"In a fucking coffin!" someone else shouted.

"Well, aren't we a cheerful bunch," Chris responded. "So we have an 'undertaker' and 'in a fucking coffin.' Perfect. And I'll just jump in here and for 'mode of transportation' say 'Chariot of Death.' You like that one, do ya, you walking sacks of skeletons? Ahahaha. Now watch us as we use your suggestions in a totally improvised skit for your comedy pleasure."

As with most improv troupes, The Five and Dime were not particularly funny or imaginative, so instead of coming up with something new on the spot, they usually just inserted the audience's suggestions into one of their standard, pre-rehearsed bits.

"Are you a good undertaker or a bad undertaker?" Bernie asked, approximating the melodious cadence of Billie Burke's good witch.

"Why, I'm not an *undertaker* at all," Chris replied, in what was supposed to be Judy Garland, but which—despite years of tutelage from Jim Bailey—sounded more like the Frugal Gourmet. (Remember him, folks?)

"Why, I'm Dorothy, the meek and mild," Chris continued. "I was dead and buried back in Kansas, on account of . . . um, the croup, when suddenly a twister came up and, um, unearthed my . . . *fucking coffin*, and dropped it here in the land of Oz, and look, it landed right on top of the bad *undertaker* of the East!"

And with that, they all sang "Ding dong, the bad undertaker's dead," and paraded gleefully around the club like munchkins. The finale, which had Elliott floating back to Kansas in a hot air *chariot of death*, could not have come soon enough.

Needless to say, they were not well received. A large man in the front yelled, "That was the biggest piece of shit I've ever seen!" then he turned to the owner. "If you know what's good for you, Neil, next time you'll hire some classy entertainment like Frank, or Steve and Eydie, or Morey Amsterdam, not bullshit like this! *Capiche*?"

Then he addressed a little guy beside him. "Chi Chi!" he cried. "La porta!"

"Yes, Big Pauly," said the little guy, who rushed to open the door just in time for the big man to storm out.

The crowd turned to look at Chris and his friends. "Hey, yous!" said the owner. "Do you cafones realize that you just chased the Chicken Man out of his own birthday party?"

"I don't care what kind of partying you guys do with your chickens," Chris said. "As long as you do it in private. Just because you're old and going to die soon doesn't mean you have to be shameless, sheesh."

But the atmosphere in the club was quickly turning menacing. The Tall Man was giving Chris a threatening stare.

"Just who do you critanos think you are?" he asked.

"We're The Five and Dime!" Chris replied nervously, as the wise guys began to surround them. "And that ain't no crime, because . . . we're all do'n time . . . drinking . . . vodka tonics . . . and lime! Help me! Somebody please help me! They all smell like olive oil and Old Spice!"

But suddenly Dellacroce was smiling:

"Well, thanks to The Five and Dime, we're rid of the Chicken

Man for the night." He took hold of Chris's neck and shook it. "I had a feeling these buffonis would do the trick. Now let's all have ourselves a real party. *Salud!*"

As eventually became clear (to posterity, if not to Chris), Dellacroce—a high-ranking member of the Gambino crew—had felt stepped over when "Big Pauly" Castellano (aka "the Chicken Man") had been named head of the family, and he'd been looking for a way to show Big Pauly some disrespect ever since. So he hired The Five and Dime to perform for his birthday. The idea was to get him so riled up that he'd have to strike back—or at least just to get him out of their hair for the night so they could have a good time.

"Pauly's a real bore at parties," said a dapper Capo, sauntering up to Elliott at the bar. "All he wants to do is talk about his freakin' corns. What are you drinking, kid?"

"Me? Oh, um, root beer schnapps, but of course!"

John Gotti laughed. "Root beer schnapps. This kid's got balls. I mean I assume he does, given dat he's male—I tink." Then he lit up a Toscano. "Sammy, get him some schnapps!"

Sammy "the Bull" Gravano hurried off to fetch it.

"Listen, kid," Gotti told Chris. "You gotta dump dat fuck'n group of yours. Day stink!"

"Now wait just a minute there, sir. You're talking about my mates, man."

"I don't care if they're your cocksucking aunt Matilda, *man*. You gotta dump 'em. I know talent, and yooz got it. Dat was the best Frugal Gourmet I ever hoid! But da rest of doz scumbags are holding you back. Dump 'em, and den maybe—just maybe—wit my help, you might get a shot at da big time."

"Right," Chris said. "I think it's time for your nap, sweetie." It still hadn't dawned on him that he was sitting in a nest of dangerous mobsters (mainly because none of them looked like Al Pacino). "Okay, let's find you someone to cut out some paper dolls with, shall we?"

But just then the front windows of the club exploded with machine-gun fire. Everybody dove for cover as shattering glass and exploding guts filled the air. The members of The Five and Dime troupe were the first to get wacked, mainly because Chris kept ducking behind each one in turn. Then Dellacroce was hit in the stomach and staggered backward. With his dying breath, he called out, "Castellano, you son of a bitch! They weren't *that* bad!" It was just by sheer luck that Gotti grabbed hold of Elliott's belt loops and Chris was able to hustle him out the back door.

"I owe you one, kid," Gotti sputtered, breathlessly jumping into his Impala. "I'll be looking out for you from now on." And with that he sped off into the night.

Chris looked down and, seeing a stream of blood trickling out of his sneaker, he passed out, and fell in a pile of dog crap.

It turned out that the bullet had only nicked Elliott's plantar wart, and although the wound was superficial, the bond between him and Gotti was anything but. The Five and Dime Massacre, as it has come to be known, marked the beginning of a lifelong association with the Mob that would both benefit Chris Elliott and cast a dark shadow over much of his achievements. Not long afterward, Gotti became the new Don, and his power reached into all aspects of New York City life—including the burgeoning alternative comedy scene—and he wasn't going to forget Chris Elliott. Within a year he had secured him a position as a tour guide at Rockefeller Center, and this being the place where NBC television was located, it was quite literally an offer Chris could not refuse.

Elliott enjoyed the work, but he wasn't particularly adept at guiding groups of tourists—some of whom spoke no English—through the endless labyrinth of art deco buildings, so it was quickly decided that he was better off stationed up on the sixty-third floor of the RCA building, selling tickets to the observation deck. The move would be a good one, for again fate was about to play an important role in his life.

The date was August 3, 1981, and Elliott was nearing the end of his day. He had sold and then resold about twenty tickets to the roof, which grossed him about fifty bucks under the table—fifty-five of which he would kick back to Gotti. He was just locking up when a lanky, midwestern guy wearing jeans and a baseball cap with a smiley face on it strode up to the counter.

"Is it too late to go up to the observation deck?"

Elliott recognized him immediately. David Letterman's morning show had just been canceled, but it was common knowledge that NBC had already promised him Tom Snyder's 12:30 a.m. time slot, and that after a final week of obligatory tapings, Dave would gear up for a brand-new show called *Late Night with David Letterman*. Chris was immediately starstruck. "Oh, I think we can accommodate *you*," he replied. "I'm a big fan, you know. Your humor is so . . . um . . . saucy . . . like a fine wine . . . or a rare bird . . . fried and then basted in Tabasco . . . that's why I use the verb 'saucy.' "

"Ah-huh. Two tickets, please." Dave pulled out a wad of cash and peeled off a hundred-dollar bill. Then he turned to the woman accompanying him. "I think you're going to enjoy this, Mother—as long as the weather holds up, and we don't get any hail the size of canned hams. Hee hee hee." The woman just rolled her eyes. She had heard the joke too many times.

"Wait," Chris said. "If this is your mother, then you're entitled to the kiddie fare. Two-fifty, please."

According to Elliott, "Letterman laughed so hard he pulled a femoral hernia."[*]

Up on the observation deck, the view of Manhattan stretched majestically out on all sides. "Right over there is the Empire State Building," Dave pointed out to his mom, "and over there is the Statue of Liberty, and right over there is the pants factory where they manufacture all the world's finest pants."

Chris snuck up behind them. "Just so you know," he blurted out, "my father is Sam Elliott, the famous cowboy humorist! And my mother is Bette Davis, the famous . . . Hollywood, um, bitch."

Dave was annoyed, but ever the gentleman. "Ah-huh. That's neat. I bet you got some stories there, huh?" Then he and his mother moved quickly to the far side of the deck.

"Right over there is the meatpacking district, Mom. I'm sure you could raise some hell down there if you had a mind to. Hee hee hee. Just joking, of course."

"Mr. Letterman, don't you think that entitles me to a job on your new show?" Chris was right behind them again. "You know . . . my parents being so famous and all?"

"Well, jeez, I don't know about that."

"I can dance! Watch this."

"That's not necessary, sir," Dave said.

Chris squatted down and wrapped his legs around his neck, and then rolled back and forth like a cannonball. In the process, he accidentally passed gas.

---

[*] Chris's, not Dave's.

"Good Lord," Dave moaned. "Yeah, I don't think we need a song and dance man on the show at the moment but thanks just the same."

"And I do impersonations, too! Listen to this beauty." Chris cleared his throat. "I shouldn't have been convicted of anything except running a cemetery without a license. That's my John Wayne Gacy. Eerie, huh?"

"Ah-huh. Look, honestly, I don't think—"

"Plus I can do *this*, watch!" Chris stuck his fingers down his throat and made himself throw up.

"Jesus Christ."

By this point Dave was so weirded out that he just wanted to get the hell off the roof, but Mrs. Letterman was charmed by Elliott's hijinks. "I think he's wonderful!" she exclaimed.

"Mother, please."

"No really, he's like Billy Barty, Rich Little, and the 'Great Regurgitator' from the Cattle Congress all rolled into one. You should hire him, David. You might get better ratings this time if you do." Then she added in a whisper, "Plus *The Watchtower* says that if we're kind to damaged people we'll get a four-car garage in the afterlife."

Chris put his arm around Mrs. Letterman. "Aw shucks, thanks, Mrs. L." And he looked coyly at Dave. "We can't argue with our moms, can we?"

Letterman glanced back and forth between Chris's pathetic, pasty face and his mother's determined expression. Then he dropped his shoulders and sighed. "Okay, fine, go see this guy," and he handed Chris a card.

"Oh, thank you, thank you so much. You won't be disappointed."

"I'm not promising anything, you understand."

"No, no. Of course not, I understand, but just to get the chance to meet with this important person is more than I could possibly have hoped for. You're an angel." Chris looked down at the card and read the name on it: " 'Barry Sand—Executive Producer.' Boy, with a snazzy name like that, I bet he's *really* smart. Thanks again, Mr. L. I won't let you down."

A tear rolled down Chris's cheek as he watched Dave leave, and he pressed his hands to his heart and took a deep, wistful breath. "My God, I love him already."

*   *   *

The new wave of comedy finally came ashore on February 3, 1982, with the premiere of *Late Night with David Letterman*. Despite questionable reviews, and even more questionable content, it was clear that the show would be a big hit, and that its host was destined to become a star. At last, the youth of America had an advocate—a co-conspirator—a man whose outward button-down appearance belied his sardonic wit, and whose mixture of sarcasm, self-effacement, and plain out-and-out silliness would become the benchmark of all smart comedy to come. And somehow Chris Elliott had managed to weasel his way onto his coattails.

Barry Sand, the short, mustached executive producer with a questionable past and equally questionable sense of humor, was at first hesitant to hire Elliott. "We didn't have any positions available for balding, bearded man-children with no talent and no skills at the time," Barry told Tom Shales, "but then I got a call from the Ravenite Social Club, and I immediately created a job for the kid." He hired Elliott as the office coatrack, but quickly promoted him to doorstop, for two hundred dollars a week. It was the least glamorous job on staff, but at least he had his foot in the door, quite literally, which was no small victory considering Bette Davis had always told him that she would never allow that to happen.

Elliott was given a desk in the men's room, and from day one he made a bad impression. He was cocky, arrogant, and incompetent. He was also overtly misogynistic (but only to the chicks). Assigned to work under Jude Brennan and Barbara Gaines, the show's intrepid production assistants, he wasted little time turning on his sleazy brand of Chad Everett charm. Although he claims in many articles to have "bedded" both of them within the first week of the show, as with all of Elliott's romantic liaisons, the women have absolutely no memory of it. (Probably because it was just that good?)

One coworker who didn't succumb so readily to Elliott's advances was a shy talent coordinator from the Midwest named Sweet Paula. Chris was smitten the very first time he laid eyes on this striking brunette in overalls and tractor boots, and he was smitten even harder the second time, when he tried to lay hands on her. (He still has the scar.) They first met in an elevator. She glanced at him with her big brown eyes and then quickly glanced away. "Well, hello there, little lady," Elliott said, getting so close that she could smell the three fish fillet sandwiches he had for lunch on his steamy breath. "And what's *your* name?" The savvy talent coordinator took the corncob pipe from her mouth, smiled sweetly, and batted her long black eyelashes. "They call me . . . *Not Interested*!" The elevator doors opened and she beat a hasty retreat. Still, Elliott was determined to win Sweet Paula over. Their brief encounter had exhumed from his heart a new and profound emotion. Was it love? The last time he thought he was in love it was with a Dorado, and that kind of love was only legal in international waters. Was this real, human-on-human love? Only time would tell.

When he wasn't flirting with Sweet Paula, clogging the toilets, or down at Lindy's getting tanked on root beer schnapps, Elliott was doing shtick for the writers, from whom he never failed to get a laugh. "He had a way of wearing you down," Gerry Mulligan recalls. "He was so desperate, and everything he did was so *lame*, but after a while you almost *had* to laugh because he was just so *unfunny*." Hal Gurnee, the director, was less charitable: "He was a real pain in the ass. He used to come into the control room and sit on my lap and ask dumb questions like 'What's a camera for?' and 'Can I come into the control room and sit on your lap sometime?' But he was so stupid that it was hard not to chuckle at the guy. Kind of like how you get nervous around somebody with no face." Even then, it was clear that Elliott was developing his own unique comedy axiom, a simple but effective one that was best described by Frank Rich of the *Times* in his raving review of *Cabin Boy*: "That which is not in the slightest bit amusing, if repeated ad nauseam, shall, in the end, equal . . . genius (apparently)."

Elliott was always on the verge of being fired, but luckily Merrill Markoe, Letterman's girlfriend at the time and the driving force behind the creation of *Late Night*, took a shine to him. It's hard to imagine what possessed her. As she puts it: "I don't know what I saw in Elliott. Maybe it's because he was so eager to please. He was like a big stupid dog, and I'm a big stupid dog fan. Also I read somewhere that he had 'bedded' me once or twice—so maybe I felt like I owed him something. Who knows?" It's ironic that Merrill would refer to Elliott as a "stupid dog," because among Elliott's responsibilities at *Late Night* was the job of auditioning animals for the Stupid Pet Tricks segment, a task he always left to the last minute. He often grabbed stray dogs right off the street, brought them up to the studio, and shoved them in front of the cameras. Here, too, it seemed like the Elliott touch was already at work, because the animals that couldn't do the tricks were more often than not the ones that got the biggest laughs. Chris couldn't help but sympathize. He was also a stupid dog who couldn't do tricks.

Just like Mulligan and Gurnee, Letterman eventually found himself with no choice but to chuckle, too, and so on February 15, 1982, Dave gave Chris his first shot in front of the cameras, in a comedy piece titled "New Gift Items." Elliott entered modeling a big pile of stinking garbage. "Our garbage suit will allow you to walk the streets of Manhattan day or night in complete safety," Dave read from his blue card, as Chris strutted back and forth for a moment and then exited the studio. Unfortunately, when the show was broadcast that night, a clumsy tape operator pushed the wrong button, and *Late Night* was blacked out just before Elliott entered. By the time the mistake had been fixed, he had already exited. Chris was mortified, and the funereal bouquet of lilies that arrived moments later only compounded his humiliation. (The note attached read: "Your best work ever—Love, you-know-who.")

The next night, Elliott was back on the show wearing the same garbage suit, only this time his face was clearly visible. On air, he explained the technical glitch, and when Letterman asked him if he had gotten any positive feedback from the studio audience, Elliott, still bitter from the night before, gave a surly response. "Yes. They said it was the funniest thing they had seen in North America." This time three million viewers saw him and heard him speak, and whether he realized it or not, he had made an impression, at least on Dave. "I realized that night that Elliott had something I could never have," Letterman remembered. "He had no talent! Hee hee hee."

What followed was a series of unintentionally surreal appearances that would have been brilliant performance art if Elliott had possessed even the slightest notion of what he was doing. Like the great Andy Kaufman, Chris could really make an audience uncomfortable, but what for Andy was the calculated effect of meticulous planning and rehearsal was for Chris just a side effect of existence. He'd been making people uncomfortable since long before he was born. The real question wasn't whether he was being unfunny on purpose, but whether he even understood that most of the laughter he was receiving was of the nervous, oh-my-God-make-it-stop variety—or if he genuinely believed that he was a comic genius. According to head writer Steve O'Donnell, a highly intelligent Siamese twin who attended both Harvard and Yale at the same time, "Ninety-nine percent of comic genius is just having the nerve to think you're *that great*, but, uh, of course I guess that other one percent is pretty important, too."

To Dave, however, it didn't seem to matter what Chris was. Even when Elliott's on-air frustration with the host's chiding turned hostile, Dave continued to laugh. Chris served a purpose on the show now, albeit just to waste network time, but as a result he was given free reign to wear down his audience. Two talented writers named Matt Wickline and Sandy Frank were charged with the unenviable task of converting Elliott's wild ramblings into something close to entertainment. With their help, he unveiled a lovable (if lame) rogue's gallery of running characters, taking inspiration from the real-life characters he had grown up with in the old neighborhood. He channeled the anxious energy of "Old Man" Angelini for the Panicky Guy, and re-created the paranoid angst of Mr. Koratzanis for his Conspiracy Guy. And he was able to convey, with surprising empathy, the forlorn nature of an outsider doomed to a life of secrets when he conjured up Roger Cambell for "The Fugitive Guy." The format of each appearance was virtually the same regardless of which character he was portraying; Elliott would pop up, say something stupid, get spooked, scream like a girl, and then run out of the studio. And even though none of these running characters were "successful" in the traditional sense of being believable, having a point, or making the least bit of sense, the audience grew to expect them, as one grows to expect long lines at the DMV, or hemorrhoids, and Chris gradually began to cultivate his own following.

It was around this time that Adam Resnick reemerged in Elliott's life when he was hired as a writer for *Late Night*. "At first I couldn't believe it was him," Chris told his landscaper in 1997. "For one thing, he wore glasses now, and for another thing, he wasn't freakishly tall anymore." Resnick claimed to have been to a Russian clinic, where he had taken part in an experimental trial for a new giantism drug, which had apparently been a huge success. His height was now only about five feet, three inches—although his curly hair added another six inches or so. But Elliott was suspicious. To prove it was really him, he made Adam show him the tattoo of Ned Beatty that they both had gotten back at Steiner. "Well, okay," Adam said, "but it kind of got distorted when I got shorter." In fact, the tattoo now looked like the double lightning bolt insignia of the Aryan Brotherhood. "But you can still make out the essence of Ned somewhere in there," he said, flexing his muscle.

"Didn't it used to be on the other arm?" Chris asked.

"Uh, yeah," said Adam. "That's, uh, another side effect of the treatment. 'Tattoo migration,' they call it. Plus you also lose any birthmarks you used to have, and all your fingerprints change."

But Chris wasn't convinced. "Tell me something only Adam would know . . . like, what got us into all that trouble back at Steiner?"

"Hmm . . . let's see. Blowing spitballs?"

"Close enough—it was kidnapping our math teacher and leaving him in a barrel to slowly die of starvation."

Adam was shocked. "We did that? That's *insane*."

"Yeah, those were the days," Chris said. "Oh, Adam, it *is* you! Long time no see!" Chris did some air kisses, but Adam just stood there and watched him like he was out of his mind. "Welcome back, old buddy, old pal, old friend of mine!"

It was like the old days all over again. The two had the run of the place, just like at school, and they promptly greased the banisters and put cheese on all the lightbulbs. Elliott fell back into his old habit of relying on Resnick for everything, just like he had at Steiner, and for his part Resnick immediately took control of his friend's career—brainstorming, devising bits for him to do on the show, and corralling willing groupies into the mop closet. No matter how befuddled Elliott got, he knew Resnick would somehow take care of things. This was the nature of their symbiotic relationship. There was nothing wrong that Resnick could not make right. Even when Chris was worried about the big premiere of his new running character, "The Guy Under the Seats," Adam had it covered.

"I sure hope I can pull this off," Chris said nervously, as he dabbed his face with Ajax. (NBC refused to waste real makeup on what they lovingly called "a lost cause.") "Don't worry," Adam told his friend, "if things aren't going well, I'll just let a squirrel loose in the audience or something."

Elliott seemed poised to blast into the stratosphere of fame and fortune. David Letterman would provide the launchpad. Resnick was back to make sure his bits hit with the audience. Plus, Irving Fichman showed up out of his past to manage his finances and help guide his career. (And even John Gotti had dropped by to generously remind Chris that he would still be allowed to keep half of everything he made— " 'Cause we're blood braders, right?")

But there was one thing still missing, and that fateful night after he had supposedly "wowed" the audience with his new Guy Under the Seats character, the missing part came a-knocking on his mop closet door.

"Yes?" he said, quickly pushing aside the lilies and boiled Lobster Gram from his mother.

Sweet Paula stuck her head in. "Nice dressing room," she said.

"It's really more the mop's," replied Chris. "I'm just keeping it warm."

"I just wanted to tell you great job tonight."

Chris grinned. "It was pretty mind-blowing, wasn't it?"

"Well, I wouldn't say mind-blowing, exactly . . ."

"I mean, the crowd went nuts! And everybody was saying I was a genius afterward. And if everybody says it, then it must be true, right? Because only a genius could make that many people think a moron like me had any talent."

Sweet Paula silenced him with a finger to his lips.

"I think you were very charming out there," she said, and gave him a gentle kiss on the cheek. "Just do me a favor."

"Name it."

"Don't turn into one of those insufferable Hollywood phonies."

"Never."

SEVEN

Over the course of the next few years, *Late Night* viewers grew accustomed to Elliott's freaky appearances. His innate ability to blur the lines of reality with self-serving walk-ons and gross stunts (like eating dog food or drinking cooking oil) often baffled even the show's savvy host, but his audience couldn't get enough of them. The idea had taken root that Elliott's moronic bits were actually meant as performance art, and Chris was rapidly becoming the Pied Piper for a whole generation of disillusioned youth, who regarded his humorless work as nothing short of genius. Due largely to Adam Resnick's repackaging of the Chris Elliott "brand," he insinuated himself within the fringes and tassels of our cultural fabric. *Time* magazine labeled him "an imbecilic prophet and poet—the moronic equivalent of Bob Dylan." Yet he was still restless. He yearned for more. He wanted to push the envelope—but when he first appeared as Marlon Brando in the summer of 1987, he did more than that. He eliminated both the envelope and the stamp, and audaciously delivered the "Marlon" character COD. The audience realized right away that they were witnessing something altogether different.

For starters, Elliott now looked to weigh close to three hundred pounds. In preparation for the role, Resnick had insisted that Elliott gain weight. Resnick was a stickler for details and now that he had taken control, he wasn't going to let his friend's svelte washboard stomach stand in their way. So taking a cue from his good friend Robert De Niro, who had recently consumed gallons of beer and ice cream for his role as Jake LaMotta, Elliott bulked up for Brando by eating quarts of tartar sauce and drinking a six-pack of schnapps a day.

Rehearsals were grueling. For months Elliott and Resnick camped out at the Harlequin Studios in Times Square, a decrepit rehearsal space infused with the pungent redolence of stale urine. There they wrote dialogue, tested out wigs and fake noses, and perfected the intricate choreography of the Banana Dance. Twyla Tharp was brought in to add a bit of classical ballet to the routine, but Resnick and Tharp tangled assholes, and after an agonizing day of untangling, Tharp called it quits. "To hell with this shit," she said, limping painfully home. Irving Fichman and Sweet Paula, who was now Chris's official "main squeeze" (the remaining "secondary squeezes" having found themselves squeezed out) often joined Adam and Chris at the Harlequin. Sweet Paula sat off to the side quietly reading her farm reports on a bale of hay that Chris had flown in daily from Iowa, while Fichman and Resnick cracked the whip, taking turns driving Chris through his grueling routine. "You're killing him!" Sweet Paula complained, but both Resnick and Fichman turned their respective deaf ears and blind eyes to her concerns. "Don't you understand? We're going for realism with this running character!" Irving insisted. "He's still not fat enough. He needs to be fatter! That's what the people want nowadays! Look at Nell Carter—she's a huge hit and why? Because she's fat, fat, fat."

Elliott's physical transformation was alarming on its own, but the characterization itself was even more disturbing. In the past, the "great absorber" had captured something of the essence of Jay Leno, Marv Albert, and Morton Downey, Jr., but nailing the subtle intonations of the world's most iconic American actor proved more daunting. Elliott threw himself into the role like never before. Every day, he adopted more of the belligerent attributes of the real Marlon Brando. His own personality merged with that of the famous actor's, and the lines between fantasy and reality grew ever more vague. Once when Sweet Paula and Chris were denied a table at Bagel Nosh, a fancy Upper East Side eatery, Elliott exploded. "Do you realize who you're talking to?" he fumed. "I'm Marlon fucking Brando!" and he belted the maître d' in the mouth and threw him through the giant rotating bagel in the window. As was the norm in those days, whenever Elliott "acted out," Fichman would pay for all the damage, deducting the cost from Elliott's paychecks—and if any feathers remained ruffled, John Gotti would step in and deal with them his way.

Finally, after almost a year of preparation, Elliott and Resnick were confident that they had something to satisfy their increasingly discerning fan base. The time was right to unveil their new creation. So on June 8, 1987, David Letterman allowed them to present "Marlon" to the *Late Night* audience.

Like "The Guy Under the Seats," it was an unforgettable debut.

Paul Shaffer struck up the theme to *Superman* and "Marlon" shuffled into the studio through the blue doors. He looked confused and deranged—like a homeless man someone had dumped off at NBC to ease the burden of an overcrowded shelter somewhere. He wore baggy pants, a Polynesian shirt, and a Hopi necklace. His hair was a disheveled bird's nest, and on his feet he sported a pair of squeaky huaraches. An aquiline proboscis jutted from his plumped-up face like Mr. Potato Head's, and he was clutching a crumpled old shopping bag—the contents of which would remain a mystery for the time being. As he strolled over to home base, he appeared to be babbling to himself, although it was difficult to make out anything coherent other than the word "mustard." He greeted Dave graciously, and then sat down grinning at the audience like a happy chimp.

The first joke out of the gate was a dud, and the requisite discomfiture that complemented all of Elliott's appearances quickly set in. Marlon presented Dave with a letter—"because," as he explained, his voice laced with an adenoidal inflection, "I hear that you are the *Letterman*. So here's a letter—man." He looked to the audience for approval, contorting his face as if asking, "Wasn't that funny, folks?" Then he cackled idiotically at his own joke.

Crickets.

After more banter with Dave, including a story about *almost* being poisoned to death by his loyal manservant Jakunta (whose name Letterman had fun mispronouncing), Marlon requested a foot massage. When Dave declined, Marlon instructed Paul (whom he called Ringo) to "rattle his cans." Shaffer played "Alley Cat," and Marlon jumped up, pulled out a bunch of bananas from his shopping bag (mystery solved), tossed them on the floor, and commenced the gyrations that would become the signature dance moves of this now beloved running character. He shuffled around, circling the fruit just the way Brando had taught him on the island, and he delighted the audience by punctuating each downbeat of "Alley Cat" with a deliriously ecstatic declaration of: "Bananas!" (something Elliott and Resnick had hoped would appeal to the youngsters in the crowd).

When he was finished, he took a bow and started to exit the stage, but before he could get past the blue doors, Dave asked Marlon to explain to the audience exactly what they could expect from this new running character.

"Well, Dave, I will be coming out from time to time to lend an air of unpredictability and awkwardness to the proceedings. All I ask is that your audience accept me for who I am." (A remarkably revealing statement that could have applied to either Elliott or Brando at the same time, or anybody else for that matter.) Then he added, "Your audience will have to make a choice: they are welcome to laugh at me, or if they prefer, they may just sit quietly and enjoy being baffled." To which Letterman quipped, "So, it's pretty much like all your other running characters then, right?" The studio audience laughed hard at Dave's joke. It wasn't scripted and there was nothing written for Chris to come back with, but Marlon would not be outdone. He immediately feigned being struck by an arrow and grimaced in mock agony. "Ow," he shrieked. "He just *zinged* me! He's a comedy porcupine!" The audience laughed harder at Marlon's ad lib than they had at Dave's zinger—which did not go unnoticed by the host. Then Marlon turned, smiled warmly, and declared, "And with that, my dear, sweet audience, I must now leave." Paul played the *Superman* theme again, and Elliott's newest running character shuffled out of the studio and into the history books, leaving behind a stupefied host and a helplessly enchanted studio audience.

Dave had been wrong. This was *not* at all like his other running characters. Up until now, Elliott had but mollified his squealing fan base with vapid running characters that he callously referred to as "clit teasers and crowd-pleasers," but now he was on to something altogether different. True, the audience hadn't reacted as frenetically as they had to the Guy Under the Seats (mainly because Adam forgot to bring his squirrel to work that day), but then again this wasn't your average bubblegum character served up to the prepubescent bobby-soxers of the eighties. This was something new and fresh, foreshadowing the more complex and more incoherent running characters of the nineties. It was brash, risky, and far less funny than anything Elliott had mounted in the past—and of course that was what was so damn audacious about it.

"The great absorber" had caught the erratic lunacy of the eccentric actor with unqualified precision. The fans out there had to have felt a transformation in their hero. With "Marlon," Elliott had shaken off the frivolous excesses of his reckless youth and joined ranks with the serious actors of the day, like Tori Spelling. He was leading the audience into uncharted territory, and as always, his fan base would have to work hard to keep up with him. Elliott's "acoustic" sound was now suddenly relegated to the dusty archives, because for better or worse, he had just "plugged in."

The Marlon character would give critics and fans alike much to mull over. It was the most deconstructed running character in the history of television, next to Goober from *The Andy Griffith Show*, the Great Gazoo from *The Flintstones*, and KITT from *Knight Rider*. Gone was the stark minimalism marking Elliott's earliest incarnations. Instead, he had presented the viewing audience with an in-depth study of a dark, tortured soul—the antithesis of himself, really—yet so faithful a depiction as to suggest the very thing that Resnick and Elliott hoped to avoid by creating it.

Rona Barrett wrote:

> Clearly, no one could have conjured up the true essence of the elusive personality of Marlon Brando—with such demonstrative ardor—having not had firsthand experience with the man himself—or more likely having had some sort of violent encounter with the actor's notoriously voracious, bisexual appetites. Possibly during a certain two-man performance of *A Streetcar Named Desire* . . . ?

Barrett had led the charge in spreading malicious rumors about Elliott ever since he first began appearing on *Late Night*. She just didn't care for him much, but in her defense, Chris could have that effect on people. Either you loved Chris Elliott or you hated him, and Barrett was definitely in the *Boy, do I hate that ugly Chris Elliott guy* camp, which first opened in the summer of 1982 with only a handful of campers but grew rapidly to become one of the most popular summer camps in the entire Western Hemisphere (despite all the murders at the lake).

Resnick had hoped that making light of Brando would put an end to the Rona Barrett style of reckless speculation, but unfortunately Elliott's performance was raising more questions than it was settling, and Barrett's snarky columns began to look like snarky attempts to embarrass him into some sort of admission of guilt.

Chris, however, had his own personal reasons for doing the character: By reducing Brando to a buffoon, he would rid himself of the emotional damage that still plagued him. He knew that to truly free himself from the Tetiaroa nightmares, he would have to face his demon—or pretend that he *was* his demon (one surmises).

As usual, Dr. Adler explains it better than anyone:

We've all heard the stories: A person afraid of snakes adopts a pet boa constrictor. Someone with a fear of great white sharks agrees to be lowered into the murky water—and a person marooned on a remote island who is attacked by a famous actor while performing the bedroom scene from *A Streetcar Named Desire* in front of a bunch of angry natives often takes on the persona of the famous actor himself. The same principle applies here: If Elliott could assume the personality of Marlon Brando, then *he* (Elliott) would become the aggressor instead of the victim. The resulting catharsis would purge him of the emotional bilge that was still weighing him down . . . along with those newly acquired bitch-tits which were probably weighing him down even more.

Undoubtedly, this drastic act of psychological self-preservation would have succeeded had it not been for one simple fact, unbeknownst to anyone at the time, not even Dave himself: Due to events that transpired just before he was scheduled to appear, Chris Elliott did not actually perform the Brando character that fateful night.

Elliott had been pacing his dressing room floor, nervously awaiting Biff's call to the studio. He was feeling extra pressure. If "Marlon" were to bomb, it could spell the premature death of a promising young career. Several good luck telegrams—from the Beales of Grey Gardens, Jim Bailey, John Gotti, Kathie Lee Gifford, and President

Ronald Reagan, among others—cluttered his makeup counter, but Elliott had barely glanced at them. Even the ominous-looking one, the text of which had been meticulously clipped from newspapers and magazines to hide the true identity of its author (a service Western Union offered back then at an exorbitant cost) escaped his full attention. The message simply read:

YOU'RE A DEAD MAN!

—Andy Kaufman

(Or something like that.) Elliott had received many such telegrams from Kaufman and would receive many more. He just assumed they were supposed to be funny. No, instead his attention had been totally consumed by the familiar bouquet of white funereal lilies, and the card on the flowers, which read:

Dearest Moron,

Against my better judgment, I plan on watching your little performance tonight. Don't fuck it up! Otherwise your "career," if you can call it that, will probably be over.

Your loving mother,
Bette Davis

Chris's shit froze. The card slipped from his fingers and dropped to the floor. His face drained of all color and he began to shake uncontrollably. He peered into the mirror in front of him and, looking at his reflection with complete self-loathing, mouthed, *You're a fake. You're a fake. You're a big fat fake!*

All the insecurities from his childhood flooded his soul and he repeated over and over again, "I can't do this. I can't do this."

He felt dizzy. The room began to spin and he thought he heard voices.

"Chris . . . Chris . . . Chris . . ."

In the mirror, Elliott saw the ghosts of The Five and Dime improv troupe standing behind him. Each member was fettered in heavy chains—the proverbial chains they had forged in life because of all the lame *Wizard of Oz* improvs they had performed.

"Chris, you can do this," Bernie Berkley said, sounding like Jacob Marley. "Just remember, the golden rule to good improv is 'Never say no—never negate'!"

"No, no, I can't!" Chris whined. "And by the way, I think saying 'no' is way funnier than saying 'yes,' asshole!" and he picked up a jar of Tuck's medicated rectal pads and smashed the mirror with it.

There was a loud knock at the door, and Biff Henderson's voice came from the other side saying, "Five minutes, Mr. Elliott. Five minutes."

Adam bounded in. "Well, it looks like a full house out there!" he announced. "Are we ready?" He looked around—but no Chris. He heard whimpering coming from behind the sofa, and he found his friend cowering on the floor in the corner, a blithering wreck, tears and mascara running down his cheeks.

"I can't go out. I can't do it."

"Of course you can. What are you talking about?"

"They all think I'm something I'm not. But my mother knows exactly what I really am. A fake! And a failure. I can't do this. I just can't do it! Oh God, I need some tartar sauce. I need a hit of tart! Are you holding? If you got any, hook me up, man!"

"Okay, okay, relax. Relax." Adam pulled out a small vial and stuck it under Elliott's nose. "This is the good stuff, kid—Mrs. Paul's."

Chris covered one nostril and inhaled. It seemed to settle him for a moment, but then the panic set back in.

"You have to go out there for me, Addy," he insisted, grasping hold of Resnick's wrist. "I can't do it!"

"No way," Adam shot back. "I'm not an actor!"

Then another voice said, "Any problems in here?" It was Irving Fichman, who was standing in the doorway.

"He's falling apart," Adam told him. "I think that witch Bette Davis had something to do with it."

Biff stuck his head past Irving. "Three minutes. Three minutes, please."

"Yeah, yeah, yeah. We'll be ready." Irving shoved Biff out of the room and shut the door. Then he squatted down by Elliott. "Kid, you gotta pull yourself together. I don't want to put any pressure on you, but if you fuck up, it could be the end of everything."

Fichman's words served only to heighten Elliott's panic, and he began to hyperventilate. Resnick looked around for a paper bag but there was none available, so he gave Chris a dirty sock and told him to breathe into it. Unfortunately, the sock had a hole in it and didn't help him much, but it made a funny photo at least. (Luckily, Fichman had his Minox with him.)

"Come on, kid. Snap out of it." Fichman shook Elliott's shoulders.

"I can't do it!" Chris insisted, and at that moment his stomach began to gurgle, and then just about every bodily function known to man exploded out of him and shot across the room in all directions. (His frozen shit from earlier made a huge hole in the drywall.)

"Wow. Never seen that before," said Irving as he toweled off.

"He's right!" Sweet Paula confirmed, shutting the dressing room door behind her. "I've seen this before. He can't go on." She knelt down and cradled her boyfriend in her arms, wiping away the tears, mascara, vomit, snot, saliva, phlegm, and some other stuff she couldn't even begin to identify.

"Don't make me do it. Don't make me do it!" Chris pleaded.

"There, there, now," soothed Sweet Paula. "No one's going to make you do anything. I'm here now. I'll take care of you."

Resnick and Fichman exchanged looks. They were a little concerned about how much control Sweet Paula seemed to have over their boy. She produced a little bottle of schnapps and attached a rubber nipple to the end of it and stuck it in Elliott's mouth. (Apparently Adam was Elliott's "tartar mule," and Sweet Paula was his "schnapps pump.")

After a moment, Chris calmed down and Sweet Paula glanced up at Adam, her expression clearly stating the obvious.

Resnick stamped his foot. "But I've never performed a day in my life!"

"That's not true," Chris belched through the sock. "You played the bean stalk in *Mother Twaddle* at Steiner. Remember? Back when you were tall and your tattoo still looked like Ned Beatty and was still on the other arm?" Then he went back to his bottle.

"Ten seconds, please, ten seconds," announced Biff.

"We don't have time to debate this," pronounced Sweet Paula, plopping the Brando wig on top of Resnick's head. "All you have to do is read the friggin' idiot cards!"

"But what if I fail? I'm not sure I could live with myself if I fail."

"Oh Christ, not another insecure actor!" Fichman smeared sweat from his brow. "Doesn't anybody in show business have any *balls* anymore? I mean, *I* don't—but not because I'm insecure. I left my balls on Omaha Beach, thank you very much."

At that moment, Chris—intoxicated and on the verge of complete delirium—began to sing, "I left my balls on Omaha Beach." (To the tune of "I Left My Heart in San Francisco.") Sweet Paula shushed him.

From the other side of the door came Biff's anxious voice. "Five seconds, please. Five seconds!"

Sweet Paula assured Adam that if he bombed, the audience would just assume it was Chris Elliott out there. "He always bombs. They won't know the difference."

"Shut the fuck up, Bernie!" Chris shouted. The ghosts of The Five and Dime were still haunting the dressing room. He threw his bottle of schnapps straight through one of them and into the broken mirror. The bottle shattered and he started crying again. Sweet Paula quickly produced a Binky and stuck it in Elliott's mouth.

Biff pounded the dressing room door. "We need Chris Elliott backstage now! I am not joking with you dumbass honkies. We need him *now*! One second to Marlon's intro. One second, please."

Adam had no choice. He quickly donned the Brando makeup, and with no more than a sixteenth of a second to spare, he made his entrance.

Luckily for Elliott, his friend's performance that night was flawless. Adam knew all the lines and all the moves by heart. Not even Letterman realized that it was Resnick out there. Of course, *everyone* should have known something was up when Dave went off script and began ad-libbing. The real Chris Elliott would have stuttered and hemmed and hawed, and with nothing funny to come back with, he probably would have just fainted. But because it was Adam out there instead of him, Marlon came back with that killer line, "He's a comedy porcupine!" which positively slayed the audience.

Had Elliott actually performed Brando that night, then he might, as Dr. Adler suggested, have cured himself of those persistent nightmares and the emotional baggage attached to his experiences on Tetiaroa, but not only was Chris Elliott *not* the one performing that night, but whenever "Marlon" appeared on *Late Night* thereafter, it was *always* Adam Resnick.

After his performance, Adam (as Marlon) exited the studio and rushed backstage to Chris's dressing room. A moment later, Elliott emerged wiping makeup from his face—the recipient of glowing accolades from his adoring fans, who seemed satisfied if not overjoyed by this new running character. And so the famous hoax began.

Like so many lies in Chris Elliott's life, the subterfuge was born out of his deep-seated fear of success, his stage fright, and his personal insecurities. He was cheating again. He didn't even have to, but he was. It was just like copying off Resnick's test papers back at Steiner, only this time it was network television and the stakes were considerably higher. This was a dangerous game that would have to be kept a secret at all costs.

It would have only been a one-time deal, with Elliott mustering up the courage to appear as Brando the following week, were it not for the mystique that grew up around the character. Of course, right away there were doubters and questions as to whether or not it was really Chris Elliott or someone else pretending to be Chris Elliott pretending to be Marlon Brando, but that only elevated the bit from one of Elliott's standard, surreal creations into a piece of truly edgy performance art. The general consensus was that it had to be someone else under that heavy "Marlon" makeup, but no one really knew for sure, and nothing could ever be proven. The public, finding the mystery simply delicious, ate the whole thing up—then regurgitated it several times, and ate it up again.

Adding to the confusion was the fact that occasionally Elliott really *did* appear as Brando—never on the show, despite what some staff members still think to this day—but at mall openings, children's birthday parties, and whenever he ate at Bagel Nosh.

If Irving Fichman booked Elliott to do the Marlon character at a venue other than *Late Night*, Chris always insisted on two separate hotel rooms—one for him and one for Marlon—and sometimes when Elliott performed at colleges, he would confound the audience by first announcing that he was about to do his famous Marlon character, then walking off stage only to reenter five seconds later as "Marlon." *Obviously it had to be somebody else*, they thought. *But who?*

Yet Marlon and Chris Elliott never appeared together, which kept the door open to the possibility that somehow—some way— maybe it really was just Chris Elliott and he was pulling off some flawless illusion—perhaps taught to him by his good friend and fellow tartar-sauce addict Doug Henning, the semi-famous and incredibly ugly magician. As with the pranks they pulled back in high school, Resnick and Elliott enjoyed watching the audience scratch their heads trying to figure out how the gag was accomplished.

To this day, there are even a few people who think it was actually Brando himself. Believe it or not, documentation exists to support this theory: in a letter addressed to the cremation urn containing the ashes of his dear friend Wally Cox, dated November 3, 1987, the real Brando wrote: "Hiya, Cox. Coming east soon—very hush-hush. Can't wait to do Elliott again." Although the phrase "can't wait to do Elliott again" is open to interpretation, there is widespread belief among the conspiracy fanatics that Brando—the ultimate trickster—helped Elliott and Resnick by appearing as *himself*. If this were true, then it would have been Marlon pretending to be Adam Resnick pretending to be Chris Elliott pretending to be Marlon. However, it's doubtful that Brando would have played along unless he was also pretending when he vowed to kill Elliott for deflowering his bride back on Tetiaroa. . . .

The Brando character was a phenomenal success, and the Banana Dance swept the country. Along with the Truffle Shuffle, it was the most popular dance craze of 1988. Knowing that the character's continued success relied on complete secrecy, Adam asked for and received a bigger cut of the take, which bought his silence and secured the deception. For his part, Elliott was happy just to bask in all the glory, and there was plenty of glory to be had. According to the press of the day, the heir apparent to the Davis-Elliott dynasty—the scrawny little kid from the tough Upper East Side who used to flush lobsters down the toilet, and who had spent the better part of his childhood pretending to be blind—had finally made good.

Rolling Stone wrote: "If The Guy Under the Seats was Elliott's 'The Reflex' by Duran Duran, then 'Marlon' was truly Chris Elliott's 'Theme to Arthur.'"

But at the very least "Marlon" would become Elliott's "Mildred Pierce," and Chris would finally become what he always dreamed of becoming, and what Bette Davis had always told him he would never be: a bona fide D-list celebrity.

EIGHT

Despite Sweet Paula's admonition, Elliott's fame went straight to his head. As the accolades came pouring in, it became increasingly clear that he would no longer be seen as just another member of Letterman's calvacade of dim-witted monkeys. No, from now on he would be known as a "dim-witted monkey extraordinaire"—an honor bestowed on him personally by the New York Zoological Society, which after extensive examination had determined that he was in fact an "ape apart from others" (much to the relief of New York's ape community, which was tired of having to invite him to all their functions). After the premiere of "Marlon," Irving Fichman was inundated with more offers for his client than he could possibly handle, and with Dave's blessing Chris began to dip his simian paws into the scum-filled pond of show business that lay beyond the relative safety of the *Late Night* landscape.

He began by doing bit parts on shows like *Jay Jay and the Sparkleberry Tree*, *Gullah Gullah Island*, and *Zoobilee Zoo*, ironically playing dim-witted monkeys on every one. He was more comfortable hiding in the furry costumes, where he was safe and sound and didn't have to expose his true lack of ability. But just as Jim Morrison needed coaxing from Ray Manzarek to finally turn around onstage and face his audience, Elliott needed coaxing to ditch the stupid monkey suits and face his (also by Ray Manzarek, who went on to have a successful second career coaxing insecure nut jobs out of the various shells in which they were hiding). As a result, Chris finally appeared as a human being, first on *Miami Vice*, then *The Equalizer*, and then on Jackie Gleason's *American Scene Magazine*. These early appearances, although brief, made a splash, if for no other reason than that nobody with such a weak chin had ever been allowed in prime time before. Sensing a possible weak-chin trend, it wasn't long before Hollywood came knocking.

While still under contract with Letterman, Elliott signed with MGM and took supporting roles opposite Raphael Sbarge in the teen comedy *My Man Adam*, and opposite Paula Poundstone in *Hyperspace*, an early *Star Wars* parody. "It wasn't a smooth transition to the movies for the kid," Poundstone recalled. "The studio insisted on using a face double for all his close-ups, and they hated his voice, which sounded a lot like Mayor Bloomberg, so Glenn Close looped all his lines." Although neither *My Man Adam* nor *Hyperspace* was ever released, word at MGM was that Elliott was a *comer.* In the popular Hollywood vernacular of the day, a "comer" was somebody to watch, to keep an eye on, somebody who was going places fast, as well as somebody who ejaculated rapidly, like at the drop of a hat—any kind of hat, even like a porkpie hat or one with a propeller on top. Bigger roles quickly followed. Metro lent him out to 20th to play an FBI agent in Michael Mann's thriller *Manhunter*, based on the novel *Red Dragon* by Thomas Harris, which itself was an adaptation of the *Adventures of Beanie and Cecil Go to Sea* by Bob Clampett. Then he snuck over to Warner Brothers where he played an alien blowfish in James Cameron's *The Abyss*. After a string of lighthearted musical flops back at MGM, including *Koo Koo for Cocoa Puffs*, based on the popular breakfast cereal, in which Elliott costarred for the first time with Shelley Winters—which of course launched the tempestuous on-again, off-again affair that would span a decade and come back later in life to bite him in the ass (quite literally)—the studio accidentally lent him out to Meineke, where he worked for a year trying to install mufflers. When that little mistake was finally discovered he was quickly sold to Universal to play a hotel thief in Francis Ford Coppola's underrated contribution to the *New York Stories* film trilogy called Life with Zoe, which was in fact written by Coppola's daughter, Sofia, who was only five years old at the time and had just taught herself how to type.

Chris suddenly found himself on a treadmill. Every day was marked by the same relentless routine: he rolled out of bed before dawn, stumbled into his bathroom, lit up a Gitane (his latest addiction), and jumped into a piping-hot tub of lard. Then after downing a few nips of schnapps and popping a handful of Mrs. Paul's tartar pills (a more concentrated version of the over-the-counter stuff), he slathered his entire body in motor oil, which gave him the swarthy, macho appearance he had longed for ever since he first saw *Shaft*. He punctuated each morning's ritual by examining his reflection in the mirror and announcing sardonically, "It's showtime!" Despite the bravado, he was still insecure. He knew that he was not what he appeared to be, and that at any moment he might be found out and run out of town on a rail, or even worse, on Delta, or even worse, that he might be made to feel embarrassed—his biggest fear in life, next to his irrational fear of singer Anthony Newley. The fortitude required to maintain the façade was taking its toll both mentally and physically, plus the motor oil was starting to seep into his bloodstream, so it's no surprise that the seeds of his eventual collapse had already taken root, even before his career reached its ultimate pinnacle of moderate success.

Still, these were heady days, as anything even remotely connected with *Late Night* could always draw a crowd. "I'll never forget seeing Paul Shaffer signing autographs for a handful of fawning priests wearing *Late Night* shirts in front of St. Pat's," Elliott recalled, "and also seeing Larry 'Bud' Melman being mauled at the zoo by a group of crazed polar bears, their giant heads crowned by *Late Night* baseball caps." Now Elliott himself couldn't walk down the street without turning heads. Groupies threw themselves at him. He was usually able to avoid the big lumbering ones, but the smaller, quicker ones always hit their mark. Affair after affair followed, although they were mostly one-night stands, as no one—no matter how big a fan—wanted to put themselves through that kind of living hell twice. Still, all this extracurricular activity put a strain on his relationship with Sweet Paula. She was no idiot. She knew when a front-page photo of Chris and Shelley Winters making out at The Ivy appeared in the *National Enquirer* under the headline CHRIS ELLIOTT CHEATS ON SWEET PAULA AT THE IVY that there must be a reasonable explanation, but she was getting tired of making excuses like "I'm sure he just left his

ChapStick at home and was being nice by sharing what he'd already applied to his own lips with Miss Winters." Fearing that his one true love, the woman who bathed him, fed him, and strapped him into his bed each night, might leave and take her schnapps with her, Elliott worked up the courage to propose marriage.

The setting could not have been more romantic. Chris was actually in the hospital having an emergency transfusion after his blood motor-oil level dropped below the fill line. He dimmed the lights in his private room and lit some candles, chilled a bottle of Veuve Clicquot, and brought in a quartet to play the Pachelbel. Then shortly after being helped to relieve himself by one of the night-duty orderlies, he loudly exclaimed, "Hey, what's this shiny thing in my bedpan?" Sweet Paula, who'd been waiting dutifully at his side, watched as the reluctant orderly (as rehearsed) reached in and retrieved a fourteen-karat engagement ring—inscribed *For my darling Bette, Love forever Gary Merrill*. The orderly disinfected it and handed it to Chris, who got down on one knee to Sweet Paula and, batting his eyelashes, asked, "Would you do me the honor?"

"Are you asking me what I think you're asking me?"

"Honey, when I accidentally swallowed that thing—back when I was like four—I vowed then and there that I would wait to pass it till the right person came along. There's no doubt in my mind that you be that right person."

Sweet Paula was swept off her feet by the romance of it all. She couldn't help but accept, and the two were quietly married in the spring of 1988. So as not to diminish Elliott's bad-boy reputation with the biker set, or his lizard-king-sex-symbol status among his five adoring female fans, it was decided to keep the nuptials a secret.

The wedding was a simple but tasteful affair held at the Harlequin

Rehearsal Studios. It was attended by only a handful of friends and family, as well as a bunch of the dogs that Elliott was still required to audition for Stupid Pet Tricks. At the time, Sam Elliott and Bette Davis were up in Canada shooting *Out of Africa*, so Jim Bailey stood in for both of them—dressed as Sam on one side and Bette on the other. Elliott's relationship with the press had grown hostile of late, mainly because of his annoying habit of dogging their every move, so to throw them off, word went out that the big Elliott wedding would be held at St. Patrick's Cathedral at eleven o'clock, but that at the same time the Banana Splits would be reuniting at the Harlequin studios. Needless to say, the excited press skipped St. Pat's and showed up at the Harlequin en masse, but the next day's coverage reflected their rage at being duped. Dorothy Kilgallen called the wedding "the most heinous collection of inbred has-beens, homely cross-dressers, and lice-ridden canines ever to soil our precious Times Square. . . . And where the hell were Fleegle and Snorky?"

Of course Elliott remembers it quite differently. "It was a fairy-tale wedding," he told Gay Talese years later in the infamous *Esquire* article that basically killed his career. "Sweet Paula looked positively radiant, but of course I looked even more radianter." Apparently Jacqueline Kennedy was also enchanted, saying, "It was about as enchanting as a visit to the iguana house." And President Ronald Reagan, for whom Elliott had campaigned, against the wishes of his friends (as well as Reagan's own wishes), seemed equally impressed. "I thought the place smelled like you-know-what." But John Gotti really put his finger on it when he described it as "a classy affair," adding, "After da two's exchanged der vows we all went down da street and took in a couple of pornos. It's don't get better den dat."

Chris and Sweet Paula settled into a sprawling apartment on the seventh floor of the Upper West Side gem known as the Bramford (or "the Bram"). It was no coincidence that the Bram's Gothic architecture was reminiscent of San Semolina. The same architect had designed both places, as well as the Cloisters and San Quentin, and so Elliott felt right at home amid the massive arches, paneled walls, and reeking dungeons. Their neighbors, however, took a little more getting used to. Actress Ruth Gordon and her husband, writer/director Garson Kanin, lived right next door. In fact, at one time both apartments had been a single grand apartment, and there was still a closet door at the end of the Elliotts' hallway that had a door inside it that led to the Kanins' adjoining suite. Ruth Gordon's distinctive cackle could often be heard through the breach in the closet, as well as Kanin's incessant showbiz yammering, not to mention the monotonous chanting and the weird recorder music, which Garson and Ruth attributed to their friend Dr. Shand.

In addition to Chris's work on *Late Night* and his outside gigs, Fichman had Elliott (and Resnick) crisscrossing the country on a whirlwind tour with something called *Marlon on Ice*, an ill-conceived and exhausting variety show featuring a skating "Marlon Brando" backed up by a skating Nitty Gritty Dirt Band. Fichman had hoped that it would serve as a pilot for a series deal for Elliott, which of course was Chris's ultimate goal—to land a show of his own.

*   *   *

Elliottmania (if you can call it that) was at its height, and out of necessity the arms of security tightened around Chris. He was often whisked off ahead of his own entourage, and Sweet Paula frequently found herself left behind on the train platforms, taxi stands, or luggage conveyor belts.* It wasn't long before she tired of this routine and opted to stay at home. It would have been a lonely life for her had Ruth Gordon not insinuated herself into Sweet Paula's daily routine. She kept her company and the two developed a close relationship, a relationship that Chris actively encouraged. His darker side took perverse pleasure in seeing Ruth Gordon gain Sweet Paula's trust, because not long after moving into the Bram, Chris had struck up a steamy love affair with her, which thanks to the secret door in the closet, he reignited whenever he came home from the road.

Ruth Gordon's quirky zest for life struck a chord with Chris, as did her noxious old lady breath, which was apparently another of his many sick fetishes. The two were like schoolkids when they were together. They stole away whenever possible, driving around Manhattan in a hearse, listening to Cat Stevens music or crashing strangers' funerals and giggling together in the back pews. Sweet Paula supplied the stability in Chris's life—a stability that he desperately needed—while Ruth Gordon infused his days with boundless unpredictability and an abundance of nauseating sex. "I just found the whole thing so amusing," Gordon told Dick Cavett, years later. "It wasn't the sex, which was borderline torture, but the sheer danger of it all. You never knew when he was going to have one of those funny little mini-mal seizures. It was like playing Russian roulette with the guy whenever he took his pants off, and I found that just so exhilarating."

"She was a real firecracker," Elliott told Gay Talese, again in that

---

* In order to help keep their marriage a secret, Sweet Paula was packed in a duffel bag and checked curbside whenever they traveled by plane.

infamous article. "And the sex was off the hook—although not really on her part. She wore an oxygen mask for most of it, and I always wore a gas mask, but I was at the top of my game, if you know what I mean, Gay. Every which way but loose, you feel me? Well, if you're feeling me, *don't*. I don't swing that way, if you get my drift. Just kidding, but you get it, right? Because your name's *Gay*? Oh, everybody's right, I really *am* brilliant, aren't I?"

When at home, the Elliotts spent long evenings next door with the Kanins, and Sweet Paula often found herself alone with Garson in the living room, his pipe smoke a suffocating smog as he regaled her with stories of Hollywood's bygone days, while at the same time Elliott was in the kitchen knee-knocking Gordon up against the refrigerator. Sweet Paula tried to tell herself that the two were probably just putting down new linoleum. She had a hard time believing her friend Ruth could do anything so naughty behind her back, but she was well aware of her husband's growing reputation as a cocksman (although for a while she thought that just meant that he enjoyed raising chickens in his spare time). But deep down Sweet Paula knew something was going on, and she resolved to hold on to her man the only way she knew how. . . .

Despite the dismal reviews for *Marlon on Ice*, the live show still raked in the bucks, and for a time it seemed as though Chris was indeed at the top of his game. Yet the erratic behavior he was displaying in his private life was beginning to seep into the professional one, and even amid all the success there had already been some missteps that should have set off alarms.

For starters, Elliott had been conflicted about doing the role in *New York Stories*. He fretted over whether it was the right career choice for him and worried (privately) that he may not have the chops to play a convincing villain. His insecurities were not helped when Adam Resnick said he doubted that Francis Ford Coppola even knew who Chris was. Fred Roos, Coppola's producer, had hired Elliott after seeing one of Adam's appearances as Marlon on *Late Night*, and he had apparently thought that the *Godfather* connection would be a good press angle, but Francis himself had never auditioned Chris. "Coppola isn't even going to know your name," Resnick said, busting Elliott's balls. "He's just going to call you 'the guy with the beard,' mark my words."

"Of course Francis knows who I am," Chris shot back, feeling the need to defend his reputation. "And I'm certain he's a big fan. As a matter of fact, I bet he thinks I'm as brilliant as everybody else does. If you don't believe me, just read all my press." Elliott had received so many compliments on his Brando impersonation that he had forgotten whose it really was.

When the day of the shoot finally arrived, he reported for makeup and wardrobe, and sashayed around the craft service table all cool and cocky like he owned the joint. At first things seemed to be going smoothly, but then a technical glitch slowed everything down. What was supposed to be only a couple of hours' shooting dragged on into the night. Chris waited patiently in his single banger trailer (an insult in itself, because he felt that anybody of his stature deserved at least a double banger trailer, especially considering all the banging he planned on doing during the shoot), but he wasn't called to the set until about three in the morning. Exhausted from Fichman's relentless schedule—and his mind ravaged by the toxic effects of all the tartar pills and syrupy booze—Elliott stumbled onto the set bleary-eyed and loaded for bear.

Little Sofia sat on her pap's lap giggling as Daddy comically stuffed a cannoli past his beard. Elliott began to say something like "Hiya, Francis, how's tricks?" but an assistant director stopped him and coldly told him where to stand. Elliott hissed. In his mind, he was already being treated badly. Just before the cameras started rolling, Francis stood up, put little Sofia back in her writing crib, and began to re-block the scene. As he moved various actors around the set, pointing here and pointing there, he gestured at Elliott and said, "Then the guy with the beard comes over here." That was it, the last straw. Elliott couldn't believe what he had just heard. Was Resnick a witch or something? It was the ultimate insult. Chris stormed off the set and vowed never to return, but nobody noticed. It was not until many hours later when Francis was watching the dailies that he realized something was missing: "Hey, where's that ugly guy with the beard?"

Elliott's defiance lasted only about half a day. By then Fichman had been contacted by Coppola's high-powered attorneys, who had stated in no uncertain terms that if Elliott didn't return to the set he would be sued for breach of contract. Forever in fear of lawsuits, Elliott made a lame attempt to cajole Sammy "the Bull" Gravano to rough up Coppola and Roos, but Gotti put the kibosh on that plan. "You want my guys to strong-arm Francis Ford Coppola?" he said. "Da man who put us all on da map? No way. He's a genius. I mean, granted, da *Cotton Club* wasn't dat great, and *Rumble Fish* kind of sucked, and dis here *New York Stories* ting sounds like a load of shit, too, but nottin' can take away *Godfader One* and *Two*. Let's just pray he doesn't fuck it up by trying to do a *Godfader Part Tree*, am I right? Now you get back and do's yours job, or else I'll have my boys rough *you* up! Capiche?" So with his tail between his legs,

Elliott returned to the set and finished shooting out the rest of the scene. It was the first time an extra had ever walked off a Francis Ford Coppola film, but from then on, Francis knew Elliott's name—which turned out to be not such a good thing, because he made sure to never cast him in any of his future movies, which is too bad because there was a perfect role for Chris in *The Godfather Part III*, but it went to the esteemed actor and fellow sun-worshipper George Hamilton instead.

Another misstep occurred the day that *The Abyss* had its New York City premiere. During the filming down in North Carolina, James Cameron, who was known for his volatile temper, had been an ogre on the set, yet for some reason he had taken a liking to young Chris Elliott—so much so in fact that he suggested the two should do a comedy together at some future date. But then Cameron appeared on *Letterman* to promote *The Abyss*, and Elliott inadvertently humiliated him with a badly conceived comedy sketch. "Are you sure he's going to think this is funny?" Adam had asked Chris before the show. "Who, Jimmy Cameron?" Chris replied. "Of course he will. We're buds. Jimmy has the best sense of humor. He loves to laugh at himself. Trust me." Then—just before Cameron was to come out and plug his movie—Chris appeared telling Dave that he had a big role in *The Abyss* and that he'd brought a clip to show the audience. Then he ran a fake clip that showed him and fellow writer Gerry Mulligan wearing stupid-looking wet suits and sitting in the cheapest underwater set you could possibly imagine, surrounded by silly hanging plastic fish. Chris was shouting, "Help! Help! We're stuck down here in the scary Abyss and it's really scary! We can't swim! Help! Help!" The audience along with Dave howled, but according to eye-witnesses, James Cameron sat in the green room watching the monitor, quietly seething. When Elliott was done, Dave introduced the director of the real *Abyss*, who was then forced to come out, sit down in front of the still-giggling audience, and try to promote the serious piece of work that had taken him five years of his life to make. Needless to say, Elliott and "Jimmy" never did their little "comedy" together.

Soon afterward, Jonathan Demme offered Elliott a role in *Married to the Mob*, but for some reason, perhaps insecurity, perhaps ego, or maybe because Elliott was high on tartar sauce all the time, he refused to even return the director's phone calls. Fichman was fit to be tied. "What the hell are you doing?" he asked Chris. "The man is the director of the movie. You have to take his calls."

"I'm making him wait," Elliott replied. "David Letterman told me never to seem too eager. If you make them wait, they'll want you all that much more. Trust me, I know what I'm doing."

But after about a week Demme had waited all he wanted to, and the offer was unceremoniously rescinded. Obviously, Fichman was unable to control his client, and since this was still early on in Elliott's career, it didn't bode well for the future. Elliott was starting to skid out of control and nobody seemed to be able to do anything about it.

But Irving Fichman was not immune to a few missteps himself. His biggest blunder came when he decided to orchestrate a formal sit-down between Chris Elliott and Andy Kaufman. "Let's get these two whippersnappers together and see what kind of fireworks they set off." The press was invited to gather in the living room of Andy's palatial Beverly Hills home, but when Chris pulled up in his famous yellow Rolls-Royce Phantom V limousine, Andy was no-where to be found. After keeping everyone waiting for an interminable amount of time, Kaufman finally appeared in complete Elvis attire. But if the press had been expecting fireworks, they were sorely disappointed. Andy and Chris just sat awkwardly next to each other on the sofa. "Do something funny, guys!" the reporters urged, but the two were quiet and seemed uncomfortable in each other's presence.

After about twenty minutes, Elliott finally mumbled, "I'm a big fan of your work."

Another twenty minutes passed before Kaufman said, "I don't eat meat."

"I like cheese," Chris responded.

"Yes, cheese is good," said Andy, "but ice cream is the best." At which point Chris just shrugged, as if to say, *To each his own.*

After that exchange they both picked up books and quietly read to themselves until the disappointed press began to file out. When Elliott got up to leave, Kaufman stopped him at the door and in a soft voice said, "Hey, have you been enjoying my telegrams?"

"Oh, you mean all the 'YOU'RE A DEAD MAN' ones? Yes, they're very funny. Thank you."

"They're not meant to be funny."

"Oh."

"No, just kidding, they're meant to be funny."

Andy made a serious face. "Or are they?"

"Oh."

"See—that's what real avant-garde comedy feels like. All mysterious and mysteriously unsettling."

"Oh."

Andy finally lost his patience. "Just watch your back, asshole!"

Chris was by this point completely confused. "What other kind of asshole is there?" he asked. "You know—other than the one that's in the back? I mean you wouldn't want to have a front asshole, would you?"

"You will by the time I'm through murdering you . . . Or will you?"

"Can I please leave now?"

"See! You can't tell if I'm serious, can you? I AM A COMEDY GOD." Then Andy turned on his heel and walked away.

By that night, Elliott was so scared he flew to Palm Springs and back to the relative safety of Shelley Winters's generous bosom at the Four Seasons Hotel. She had made it clear to Elliott that she would happily make her bosom available to him anytime he was in town, and having been a fan of her bosom since first seeing it in *The Poseidon Adventure*, Elliott regularly took advantage of the offer. But the next day he was *really* creeped out—not only because it was the first time he had seen Shelley Winters's bosom without makeup, but because Kaufman's weird warning was still sticking in his craw. So he called John Gotti and procured for himself a Glock G31 semi-automatic handgun, which from then on he always carried—just in case.

A month passed before Elliott, now back in New York, finally got the news he had been waiting for. Peter Chernin, the smart young head of Fox television and the man who would turn out to be one of Chris's biggest supporters, called offering him a shot at his very own TV show. There was only one caveat: Chernin would only give it a green light if Chris's real parents, Sam Elliott and Bette Davis, played his fake parents on the show. This was a hard pill for Chris to swallow, and at first he said, "No way," but the more he thought about it, the more he thought it might be a great opportunity for reconciliation or revenge or whatever. It would be a gamble, but the payoff would be worth it.

Breaking the news to Dave was going to be difficult, though. Letterman had given Chris his first big break in the business. He had supported him, and even allowed him to stray from the farm with the outside projects that had offered him a chance to spread his wings, including a one-man show as Franklin Delano Roosevelt, a stint toe-dancing with the Bolshoi Ballet, and a brief tour performing the beloved toilet paper box with the world-renowned pantomime troupe Mummenschanz. In return, Elliott had always remained loyal to his mentor, to the point of maintaining his office in the men's room. Some months earlier Chris had accepted an invitation to try out for *Saturday Night Live*, and although his audition left much to be desired (he demonstrated his various double-jointed talents including an impersonation of Ronny Cox after he gets his arm broken in *Deliverance*), Lorne Michaels saw something unique in the kid and dubbed him the "anti-performer." Despite the fact that Chris would be a departure from what the *Saturday Night* audience was used to, Lorne nevertheless offered him a spot on the show. But Elliott turned it down, opting to remain with *Late Night*, which even further solidified the bond between himself and Dave. (Of course, years later Elliott actually *did* join the cast of *SNL*, where he deftly anti-performed a string of anti-unforgettable running anti-characters. But now not only would he have to tell Dave that he was leaving to do his own show, but on top of that he was taking Adam Resnick with him.

Resnick was by this point one of the show's top writers and nearly indispensable.

Laurie Diamond remembers the meeting between Chris and Letterman being emotionally charged. Dave was sitting at his desk eating his lunch when Chris walked into his office. Elliott just stood there shaking.

"What's up, buddy?" Dave asked, as he scooped a wooden spoonful of caviar into his mouth.

"Dave," Chris began, his voice quivering. "Dave, um, well, see Adam Resnick got offered the chance to create a show out in LA and he wants to take me with him."

"Great. See ya."

Of course Chris's memory of events differs somewhat. "I told Dave in no uncertain terms that I could no longer carry his show for him and that I had to go do my own thing. The poor guy begged me to stay, but I held my ground. I told him to act like a man. When I started to leave he threatened to kill me and I just laughed. 'Take a number,' I said. 'You don't have the nerve.' I was feeling pretty darn cocksure of myself at the time, on account of having my trusty Glock in my pocket, don't cha know. I hated to break the news that way to the guy, but he really needed a slap in the face, so I slapped him in his face and left."

As Chris strolled out of the *Late Night* offices for the last time, he picked up a couple of pink phone messages. The top one was from Sweet Paula. "We're pregnant!" it read. He could not have been happier. It was a dream come true. The stars had aligned. His family would move out to sunny California and he would star in his own TV show, and perhaps get to win back the respect of his mother (not really win it back, because he never had it, but you get the idea). For one brief shining moment he was on cloud nine, but then he read the other phone message. It was from Ruth Gordon. Apparently, she was pregnant, too.

About a week later he got a call from Shelley Winters's bosom, and yep, you guessed it, el-knocked-up-a-roony as well.

NINE

For Bette Davis, the prospect of going back to work in *television* was bad enough, but the notion that she would be working for her son—the son she'd once called "God's biggest joke on human beings"—was an even harder pill to swallow. Unfortunately, the aging diva would have little choice in the matter. She had received critical acclaim the year before, playing Lillian Gish's twin sister in *The Whales of August*, and Mickey Rooney's twin brother in *Bill—On His Own*, but there were no other twin roles available at the time and her future in film looked bleak. No one questioned her talent, at least not if they knew what was good for them, but she had garnered a well-deserved reputation for being difficult, and in fact—according to a confidential memorandum recently released by the justice department—J. Edgar Hoover had even put her on the "most feisty" list, classifying her as "Feisty Broad

Number One" as far back as 1930. It was a label she despised. "If 'feisty broad' is the best some peeping queen can come up with to describe me, then he's not worth the spit it takes to slob his knob." Sam Elliott's career was also faltering, as America's love affair with mustaches and red meat was beginning to wane. So it was with much humility that Davis rang up Peter Chernin and told him that she and Sam would agree to do the pilot called *Get a Life*. She didn't share Chris's hope that the project might lead to a family reconciliation and/or grudge-settling death match. She wasn't interested in either. To her, it was just another job, a way back into the business, the business that had turned its back on her, and all she cared about was getting through the dreadful humiliation she would have to endure in the process.

During rehearsals, Davis infused "Gladys," the domineering matriarch of the fictional "Peterson" family, with her own trademark style of clipped intensity, while Sam Elliott anchored the pilot's zany surrealism by imbuing the brass-necked patriarch, named "Fred," with a powerful dose of sagacious frontiersman chutzpah. Rounding off the cast was the handsome actor Sam Robards, son of Jason Robards and Lauren Bacall; and famed Broadway actress Dame Robin Riker, who had been tapped to play Chris's neighbor, Sharon. Ironically, Chris's character, "Chris Peterson"—the chubby, bald-headed thirty-year-old paperboy who still lived at home with his mom and dad—was the only one that raised a few eyebrows at the network. "I think we were all a little put off by Chris's dim-witted, man-child persona," Peter Chernin remembers. "Plus the character was a little bothersome, too."

Chernin had responded lukewarmly to Elliott's first idea for a show—in which Marlon Brando gives up a career in acting to become a nanny—but seeing as how the movie *Big* starring Tom Hanks as a boy trapped in a man's body was still number one at the box office, Chris gambled that he could sell Fox on a thirty-year-old guy who, despite a bad case of arrested development, still managed to save the day by employing naïve, childlike solutions to everyday problems—a "real-life Peter Pan," as he described him. It was how Chris had always imagined life at his parents' might have been like—the life his mother had denied him by kicking him out before he had the chance to fail to become a man and never leave home. It was supposed to be a fantasy, and Elliott did his best to stress the charming, fairy-tale aspects he wanted to give it. "Maybe I could even fly," he gleefully suggested.

"I get all that," Peter Chernin had said, "but we still feel like Chris's character needs to be more responsible. He shouldn't just be a paperboy, and he shouldn't just live at home with his mom and dad—that makes him seem too pathetic."

"No problem," said Irving Fichman. "We'll make Chris the *head* paperboy, in charge of like ten other paperboys. That gives him a real job." And Adam Resnick added, "Yeah, and instead of living at home with his mom and dad, he can live over their garage! That makes him more responsible."

Chernin seemed only slightly mollified. "Yes, but . . ."

"Crikey!" another voice interrupted. "This show sounds like *slag* to me. What we really want is the next *Cosby*." Rupert Murdoch stepped out from behind the curtains in Chernin's office. "Can you deliver that for us, mate?" Apparently, Murdoch wasn't satisfied with Fox's reputation as the edgy alternative to mainstream television. Despite the success of controversial shows like *The Simpsons*, *Married with Children*, and *In Living Color*, he wanted to upgrade his brand

and was determined to create refined, middle-of-the road programming that would appeal to a more erudite audience.

"But of course I can deliver that for you," Elliott assured him—speaking in a French accent for no apparent reason. "Who better to be zyeh next Bill Cosby zyen me?"

So the executives at Fox expected to get an urbane family show offering warmhearted, sophisticated humor—the perfect complement for their classy new hit *Babes*, about three morbidly obese women sharing a tiny apartment in New York City. Naturally, they were flabbergasted when a script was dropped on their doorstep containing absolutely no redeeming values whatsoever and skewering the very genre it professed to be part of. They recognized the bait-and-switch right away, and the endless network notes demanding more "realism" and more "heart" began to pour in.

"I don't get these bums in the gray flannel suits," Elliott complained to Pete Hamill at the Cheesecake Factory. "My blood boils when I see the mediocrities sitting on top of the TV networks."*

The incessant "noting" from the network stressed out Elliott and Resnick both. It was a constant game of cat and mouse—assuaging the network while trying to slip in the type of jokes they really wanted to do. The confusion extended even to the rehearsal process, as most of the cast were as clueless as the executives. "This is just too stupid," Bette Davis complained to Chris. "What exactly is a 'clapper' anyway, and why am I telling you to clap off the lights? You know in my day, if somebody had the 'clap,' we'd steer clear of them—give

---

* Chris actually never said that, Frank Sinatra did, but for all we know he might have been talking about *Get a Life* at the time.

'em the wide berth—if you know what I mean. 'He's a clapper,' we'd say, and then, 'Run for the hills!'"

"Well, this is the 'new humor,' Mom," Chris replied. "It's all about, uh, you know, um . . . uh . . ." He turned to Resnick. "Kid, explain the clapper joke to my mother, will ya?"

"Well, in this case, Ms. Davis, the 'clapper' isn't referring to a venereal disease, per se. It's a device that's advertised on TV. Which is funny because it's exactly the kind of joke that they would do on a stupid sitcom, only when we put our fake laugh track in, people will know that we're secretly making fun of ourselves for doing such a stupid joke. Understand?"

"Not in the slightest."

"Well, some people will laugh at the joke because they think it's funny, but smart people will laugh at the joke because they realize it's stupid—which makes it really smart."

"Because it's stupid?"

"Exactly."

"Why not just write a *funny* joke instead?"

"Because, uh . . ." Resnick seemed genuinely perplexed.

"It's, uh, too . . ." said Chris.

"Hard?" said Bette.

"Yes, very hard," they both said, nodding their heads in unison. "Much, much too hard."

"Fuck it," Davis said, throwing her hands up in the air. "I don't know what you boys are huff'n, but as long as the checks clear, I'll just keep my mouth shut and do my goddamn job."

She did her goddamn job and more. During the shooting of the pilot Bette Davis displayed the same level of perfectionism that had marked her career ever since her early days with The Little Rascals. The only dustups were between her and her female costar, Robin Riker, of whom she was immediately jealous. "I wouldn't let her piss on me if I was on fire," she said of Riker. Several valuable shooting days were lost because of their bloody catfights. Cinematographer Lucien Ballard was even forced to invent a special camera-mounted spotlight to help hide their brutal facial scars.

Yet despite the occasional discord on set, mother and son soon discovered that they shared a common vernacular—acting. Davis could no longer just sit back and snidely observe her son's work. Now she had to take regular breaks from her snideness to do some work of her own. Fortunately, she was talented enough to manage both. And like it or not, she was now working for *him*, and as such she was required to treat him with a modicum of respect. For his part, Chris was extremely protective of his mother—making sure she was never overworked, and insisting that both his parents' characters always appear in pajamas and bathrobes for their own comfort. "I don't think I really knew my mother until we started working together," Elliott told Gay Talese. "She's one 'feisty broad,' that's for sure. I can't think of a better way to describe her."

During those three weeks, Davis and Chris finally developed the respect for each other that had been so absent during Chris's formative years. Bette taught him how to drink bourbon, how to curse like a man, and also how to take a punch and to hold his breath underwater for several minutes, whether he liked it or not. "You see, son, all that so-called 'abuse' back when you were a kid was really just tough love," she explained, while dunking him repeatedly. Chris in turn introduced his mother to the joys of tartar sauce and of finally giving in to his repeated cries of "uncle." On their days off, they often drank and sparred together until they were bombed and Chris was too bruised to take any more, at which point he would climb the famous Hollywood sign—swinging back and forth like a monkey from the giant letters while Bette laughed maniacally and tried to nail him with bottles of bourbon. Those three weeks of "bonding" made up for the childhood Chris never had—or at least that's what he very loudly told anyone who asked about the scars.

Sam Elliott was overjoyed at the apparent reconciliation. One day during the shooting he stopped everything and announced, "I do declare that we are one happy family again, and that ain't no blatherskite either!"

"What do you mean, *again*?" snarled Davis, puffing away on her cig. "When the hell were we ever happy before?" And then the three of them shared a hearty laugh, which lasted about twenty minutes. They laughed so hard that they gave themselves permanent creases around their mouths, and Lucien Ballard was forced yet again to invent another special spotlight, this time to hide their hideous laugh lines.

Everything seemed to be going smoothly until the final day of shooting, when tragedy struck. The pilot script called for Chris Peterson and his mother to be trapped upside down on a roller coaster called the "Hell Loop 2000." The special-effects people had devised an ingenious plan to build a piece of track with a roller coaster car attached to it. Davis and Elliott were strapped into the car and then hoisted up about twenty-five feet off the ground, then rotated until the car was completely inverted. The plan looked good on paper, but the first time they turned the contraption upside down, Davis fell out and landed hard on her head. About six hours later, when she came to, she was fit to be tied. "God damn it, who's the goddamn genius who came up with this goddamn piece-of-shit idea?" But being a lady, she brushed herself off, downed a few shots of bourbon, smoked a pack of cigs, and climbed back into the car. This time every stagehand in Hollywood made sure that she was strapped in securely. Unfortunately, when they turned the thing upside down the second time, a 3.5 earthquake rocked the studio and Bette's seat detached from the car and fell to the ground with a sickening crack.

Everything they tried to do to make the dangerous rig work failed. Apparently it was built by the same geniuses that had built Bruce, the mechanical shark in Jaws, which never worked, either.*

Another reason the roller coaster didn't work may have been that Bette got increasingly lubricated as the day wore on, and after a while she began to slip effortlessly out of the seat, plummeting to the hard concrete below whenever the apparatus was inverted. Nobody ever thought to put a mattress underneath the thing.

By the end of the day, Chris had been hanging upside down for so long that he was hemorrhaging behind his eyeballs, and Bette Davis had received multiple concussions and was rushed to the hospital. Frustrated, and finally at his breaking point, Lucien Ballard threw up his arms, bolted off the set, and locked himself away in his attic. Ten years later, he reemerged with a new spotlight, which when mounted on top of the camera would hide *everything*—the bumps on Bette Davis's head, the scars on Robin Riker's face, and

---

* Remember hearing about that one, folks? Jesus Christ, if I have to hear Spielberg bitch about that again, I'll barf all over my Hook laser disc. We get it, the shark *never worked*!

Chris Elliott's bloody eyeballs. But apparently no one had told Ballard that the pilot had been shut down, and so the man had wasted a decade of his life. Penniless and alone, he stuck a shotgun in his mouth and blew his head off.

With Bette Davis in intensive care, shooting on the pilot ground to a halt and Elliott returned to New York City to be with Sweet Paula in time for the birth of their twins, Sweet Abby and Sweet Bridey.*

Sadly, Bette Davis never recovered, and her last words to Chris were as cryptic as they were bitter and did little to bring closure to their tumultuous relationship.

"Hey, idiot," she wheezed, gasping for air.

"Yes, Mother dearest?"

"Do you know what the word 'mediocre' means?"

"Well, I know that meat comes from cows and if memory serves me okra is a type of green vegetable, so I would assume that a meaty okra would be either a heavy, substantial okra, or a vegetable that tastes a lot like meat. Am I right?"

Bette cackled and coughed. "Yes, yes you're right. You're meaty okra—that's what you are, with a heavy emphasis on the okra or vegetable part."

"Gee thanks, Mom. I can't tell you how much that means to me to finally hear you say that."

"Listen, kid. I don't care what anyone tells you, you ain't done nothing till you see your name up in lights. That's the true mark of

* Ruth Gordon had already had her baby and had donated it to a needy family in Africa so that they could sell it to a wealthy family back here in the United States, and Shelley Winters had discovered that she wasn't pregnant after all—only bloated.

success. The ultimate. Never forget it. Once you've seen your name up in lights, there's no reason to go on."

"So afterward, I should kill myself?"

"Or before, if the spirit moves you. I'll leave that one up to you. But why wait?" and with that Bette Davis drew her last breath, closed her eyes, and passed on to that big beautiful bottle of Jim Beam in the sky.

Speculation would always remain that the repeated trauma she endured during the shooting of the Hell Loop 2000 episode of *Get a Life* had contributed to her demise, which would make sense because it was the reason she was hospitalized in the first place, but things like that are quickly hushed up in Hollywood. More troublesome, however, were the ugly rumors that began to circulate that Elliott himself had hired goons to sabotage the roller coaster. Dr. Adler puts the controversy in perspective:

There is little evidence to prove that Chris Elliott attempted to murder his mother, but he was a secretive, private figure, and not to mention practically a sociopath, given that he'd already quite possibly murdered his math teacher, driven his elderly cousins into penury and despair, vandalized an entire sleepy seaside town, molested a helpless female islander betrothed to a famous actor (after sinking an entire cruise ship), accepted help from known mobsters (after they'd gunned down his entire fellow improv troupe), forced at least one journalist to interview him at knifepoint, and taken advantage of countless infatuated groupies, including one extremely attractive psychiatrist, whose many desperate phone calls he never returned— she was just trying to help the guy in the first place—causing her to go off the deep end and devote her entire life to the study of his career. . . . Well, I wouldn't put it past him, is all I'm saying.

Certainly, Chris's reaction to Davis's death only helped fuel the scandalous rumors. As the world mourned the passing of one of the greatest movie stars of all time, Elliott flew back to Los Angeles and immediately began retooling his show.

In truth, it was the only way Elliott could deal with his grief. He did his mourning privately. He kept everything to himself. He was a loner and that's the way he liked it. He never confided in anybody. He didn't let anyone inside. In fact, he rarely let himself inside—often getting drunk and unintentionally locking himself out. He regularly complained to himself that he wasn't sharing enough with himself, and he used to get into boisterous and sometimes violent arguments with himself. Records indicate that during this period, he was frequently hospitalized with self-inflicted cracked ribs, wedgies, and painful Indian burns. He alternated between hot and cold. One moment he was a charmer—a real gentleman—and the next, he was an angry monster with an out-of-control temper. He was well aware of his Jekyll-and-Hyde personality and knew he had a real problem. "I was always amazed at how generous and loving I could be to myself," he once told himself when he thought he wasn't listening. "But then, also how cruel and nasty I could turn if I said something I didn't agree with, or if I just looked at myself the wrong way."

It's also possible that after Bette's death, Chris just wasn't capable of feeling much anymore. He was plastered most of the time. He was too numb, dumb, and full of cum to feel anything. The only thing he knew how to do was *pretend*—pretend to be talented, pretend to be sexy, pretend to be smart, and pretend to work.

And there was much work to pretend to do. The *Get a Life* pilot would have to be recast and reshot—and quickly if they still wanted to make the fall schedule, plus finding a worthy replacement for Bette Davis (and Sam Elliott, who was now too distraught to continue with the project) wasn't going to be easy.

Auditions were held at the Beverly Garland Holiday Inn on Vineland, and every established actress of the time vied for the role of Chris's mother. After each audition, Irving Fichman would escort the potential mom over to the presidential bungalow where a "casting couch" had been prepared. There, Chris would play the bartender for a while and then try to have sex with the woman. Afterward he would take her out to dinner, to either La Dolce Vita or Whomphoppers, depending on how successful his advances had been, and then possibly later on—if things were going well—dancing at The Candy Store on Sunset Boulevard, one of the many hot spots he owned with his buddy and fellow skin cancer survivor George Hamilton. Any actress who had auditioned and succumbed to his charms might be pleasantly surprised the next morning to find a dozen red roses on her doorstep, or a box of candies from Edelweiss Chocolates, or a gift certificate for a tit job, but those who didn't succumb were lucky if they got a T-shirt that said, "Wow, I'm such a loser that I gave up my one chance to have sex with Chris Elliott." Most succumbed and few complained, and only Kitty Carlisle Hart filed charges—not because of the sex, but because Chris had taken her to Whomphoppers instead of La Dolce Vita. (Though the boys from the Ravenite Social Club made sure that little scandal was kept out of the papers.)

Family portrait

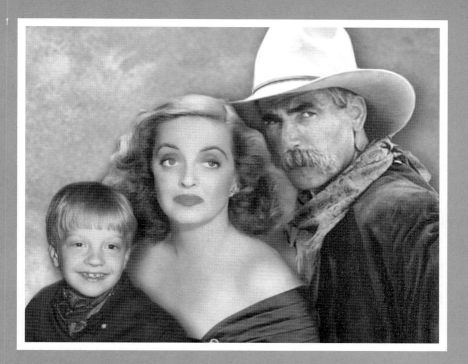

San Semolina

3

Little Chris with cousin Sook
(Big Edie Beal) at Grey Gardens

4

Lee Radziwill (Chris's
almost Summer of '42)

5

The Five and Dime Massacre

6

The infamous photo with John Gotti
at Chuck E. Cheese's

Irving Fichman—Elliott's
hotshot manager

8

Chris and the real
Adam Resnick,
photographed by Diane
Arbus (Title: "Jewish
Giant at Home with
His Best Friend, 1976")

Sweet Paula

The fake Adam Resnick
pretending to be the
real Chris Elliott
pretending to be the
fake Marlon Brando

The wedding

12

Chris with Shelley and her "generous bosom"

13

"She was a real
firecracker, and
the sex was
off the hook."

14

The Forked Cocksman
and his cronies

Aileen Wuornos, the serial
killer who almost came
between Chris and
Sweet Paula

Right: Bed-in for world
castration, with Wuornos

16

17

Elliot's billboard—what it was all for

18

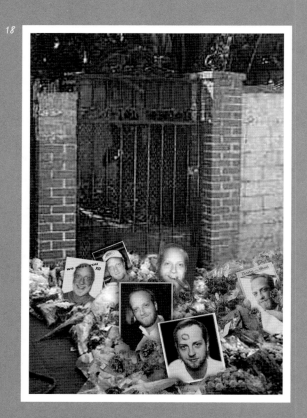

The gates at the Chateau

Casting was getting nowhere until Margie Gross, one of the many brilliant writers who worked on *Get a Life*, suggested Elinor Donahue to play Chris's mother, and in the end it was decided that the sweet, wholesome actress—the antithesis of Bette Davis—would be ideal for the role. Chris had grown up watching Donahue on *Father Knows Best*, and when he first met her in person, she seemed to command a level of respect from him that he rarely afforded his female costars. "I have to admit I had the hots for her," he told Trini Lopez when they appeared together at the Fontainebleau. "She rebuffed me during the whole audition and 'sex with the star of the show' process, but I liked that about her. The broad had real balls—Robert Young's, apparently. She kept them in a jar."

The first choice to replace Sam Elliott was Buddy Ebsen, but a week into rehearsals it was discovered that Ebsen was allergic to the silver makeup and he was forced to quit. Fichman then suggested Bob Elliott, of the popular comedy team Bob and Ray, for the role. It was a good fit, as not only did Bob look like he could be Chris's father, but his last name was similar, so only "Sam" would have to be crossed off his dressing room door—saving about three hundred thousand dollars' worth of budget.*

So with the cast finally in place, the pilot was rewritten (now with Robards and Chris getting trapped upside down on the Hell Loop 2000) and shooting on what would become a cult classic recommenced on March 1, 1990. When it was completed, the pilot tested

---

* Dressing-room-door placards were big-ticket items back then—often made out of solid gold for no apparent reason. It wasn't until about 1995 that the studios came to their senses and started making them out of cardboard.

through the roof. By July of that year, Fox had already ordered up nine episodes, and Chris and his family had relocated to Los Angeles, where everyone buckled down to shoot the series.

It's hard to tell if anyone involved with the show realized at the time that they were doing something that, in years to come, would be revered by several people the world over. Obviously Chris Elliott didn't. In fact, he acted as if he didn't even want to be there. The network grew concerned when they heard about his erratic behavior on set. He despised rehearsing, so taking a cue from his old man, he hired Jim Bailey to be his stand-in and to do all the rehearsing for him. Chris would saunter in at the last minute and say, "Where do I stand, Jim?" Before the show ever aired, he was acting as though it was a waste of his time—like he had bigger fish to fry. He was always late and always out the door as soon as they got one take in the can. He slowed the shooting process down by fooling around on the set, trying to make his cronies laugh. He had started hanging out with fellow bad boys Pauly Shore, Pee-Wee Herman, Carrot Top, and Weird Al Yankovic, and this new posse was always on the set making fart noises under their arms and cracking up during the takes.

One day, Elliott showed up drunk and insisted on playing every scene on all fours, barking like a dog. His immature clan acted as if his antics were the most amusing thing in the whole wide world. In fact, they found everything he did amusing. He had no real sense of humor to speak of, but his ego was being fed by this pack of die-hard buddies, who referred to him as Il Patrone, or the Chief, or the Forked Cocksman.

During shooting, Bob Elliott treated Chris like a son, not only on screen, but off as well. Bob's paternal guiding hand grounded Elliott and helped him get through the grueling shooting schedule. The two seemed to have much in common, despite being from different walks of life, and Bob sympathized with the young lad, who was after all just struggling to deal with the burdens of moderate success. The two forged a close relationship that would last both their lifetimes. "It was strange," Elinor Donahue remembers. "Bob Elliott seemed more like Chris's dad than Sam Elliott—they even looked alike. Hmm. Interesting. Perhaps Sam should have spent a little less time twirling rope and a little more time checking the closets, if you get my drift."

*   *   *

Get a Life bowed September 3, 1990, with a 2.5 rating and a 6.9 share, whatever the hell that means, but everyone was told that those numbers weren't bad for Fox at the time. From the start it was obvious that the show was a little off. *Get a Life* pretended that it was a sitcom, while in reality it was poking fun at the whole world of sitcoms—and maybe even poking fun at the fact that Fox had been reckless enough to give Elliott his own series in the first place. In that way, it was the perfect vehicle for Chris, who thus far had made his bones in the business by pretending to be something he wasn't. The show had successfully managed to take Elliott's anti-performance persona from *Late Night* and translate it, intact, to prime time. The response was generally positive, although before it aired, Elliott and Resnick had their doubts.

Chris and Adam braced for a rough ride from skeptical critics. Without even seeing the show, Rona Barrett had already written an advance review calling it an "abortion of epic proportions—a gigantic abortion the size of Mount Olympus—the biggest abortion in the whole wide world! Oy, but it's huge! Imagine the size of the coat hanger this one needed!" Betting that if she saw the show Barrett would change her mind, Resnick invited her to the lavish *Get a Life* premiere party—a star-studded affair held in the lobby of the Rodeway Inn on Figueroa, one of the many budget-minded hot spots that Elliott owned with partners Burt Reynolds and Ryan O'Neal. Unfortunately, inviting Rona Barrett would prove disastrous.

It was one of those stormy LA nights. Inside the Rodeway Inn, you could cut the anticipation with a knife. A large TV was set up on top of the ice machine, and cast and crew mingled about with cocktails in hand, nibbling on plates of raw tuna, which had been shaped to look like Elliott's beard (apparently the beard-shaped plates were edible, too). After all the blood, sweat, and tears that had been shed to get the show made, Resnick felt a sense of relief. Sitting alone at the bar, the teetotaler allowed himself a few sips of champagne and a rare moment of self-congratulation. It had been a long road and it was difficult for him to imagine that the show was actually going to make it on the air. Deep down part of him wouldn't believe it until he heard the opening theme—"Stand" by R.E.M.— which Chris had successfully convinced Fox would be a better choice than "Candy Man" by the Mike Curb Congregation.

At about 7:30 p.m., Chris's Phantom V pulled up in front of the Rodeway Inn. Chris stumbled out in the company of Pauly, Carrot, Pee-Wee, and Weird Al, and a cluster of wiseguys acting as bodyguards. Elliott was extremely nervous. He knew there was a lot riding on this, and so he had already been drinking for a few days before they arrived. After punching out a cameraman who wasn't even covering the premiere—he was actually just shooting B roll of a clogged storm drain for a local news story about the heavy rains— the rowdy bad boys fell into the party. Chris was immediately ushered over to the VIP table, where Sam Robards hugged him and introduced him to his mother.

"Chris, I want you to meet my mom," Sam said proudly.

"Oh, hiya, sugar tits," Chris yelled right in Ms. Bacall's face. "How's tricks? Hey, whatya say after the show you come over to my place? I got an air mattress with your name on it, baby."

Lauren was unfazed and looked at Chris with bemused, sultry eyes. "Sam tells me you're Bette Davis's kid?" she said, extending her hand. "I'm sorry for your loss. She was one in a million."

"Let's snot talk about her," Chris slurred. "Let's stalk about us." Then he gallantly pulled out his cigarette lighter and lit Bacall's fingers.

She screamed.

"Chris, what the hell are you doing?" Sam yelled, pulling Elliott away.

"I'm sorry. It's dark. I thought she had a cigarette." Elliott plopped down next to Elinor Donahue. He was already out of control when he leaned over and asked her how much it would cost to get her to "polish his knob." Donahue had no idea what that meant, but it sounded to her like the sort of demeaning housework you'd ask a servant to do, so she hauled off and landed a solid right on Elliott's jaw, which sent him flying across the table. Chris's bodyguards sprang into action, beating the crap out of Donahue, dragging her out back, and throwing her in a dumpster in the alleyway. Resnick grabbed Chris, sat him down on a stool at the bar, and ordered him a root beer schnapps.

"Now, just stay there, Chief, and don't cause any trouble. You're a little bombed."

"Righty-o, Captain." Chris saluted his friend, downed his

schnapps, and ordered another. Resnick retrieved Elinor from the dumpster, carried her back to the table, and propped her chin up on a flower vase so she'd look conscious.

Just before eight p.m., someone turned on the TV and everyone focused their attention on *In Living Color*, the show preceding *Get a Life*. This turned out to not be such a great idea. The show got huge laughs from the partyers. Although Chris was ignorant in terms of why he was semi-successful in the first place, he still had learned a trick or two about the trade, and he knew that you never follow anybody funnier than you. In fact, back at *Late Night*, Chris had always made a point of never following brilliant comedians like Steve Martin or Bill Murray or Robin Williams, or even Charlie Callas or Buddy Hackett, or anybody else for that matter, because he knew he couldn't compete. Basically he had to schedule his bits to fall after especially un-ironic tampon commercials or especially dull test patterns. But now his own show, *Get a Life*, was following the brilliant hit *In Living Color*.

Needless to say, *Get a Life* hardly got a chuckle from the crowd, not because it wasn't funny—in fact it was hilarious, I swear—but because everyone seemed predisposed not to laugh. Those who had worked on the show were pretty fed up with Elliott by this point, and they exacted their revenge by sitting quietly during the broadcast. As each silent minute passed Chris became more and more agitated. Resnick tried letting a couple of ferrets loose, but everyone just yawned. The resentment kept building up inside Chris. When it was over, the place was like a morgue. Lauren Bacall tapped Elliott on his shoulder on her way out. "Don't look so sad," she said. "It wasn't *that* awful," and then she left quickly with her son. Only one person in the back of the room was clapping, slowly. Rona Barrett. When Chris glared at her she began to laugh.

"What did I tell you?" she shouted across the room. "An abortion the size of Mount Olympus!"

That was it. Chris pulled out his Glock, aimed it at Barrett, and began shooting. Pandemonium broke out. Barrett jumped for cover. Elliott was drunk and each shot missed by a mile, but one bullet found the TV set, blowing it up, and a few ricocheted and nicked a couple of innocent tourists to death. One of Elliott's bodyguards grabbed the gun from his hand and pushed him out the door.

"Get out of here, pal. Run, man, run."

Elliott ran out into the rainy night and disappeared into the gloom. Like so many other times in his life, he ran—and ran and ran. Chris was an expert at running—at running away from problems at least. Actual running made him want to throw up after about half a mile. Eventually he found his way to the Santa Monica Pier and contemplated jumping, but he didn't have the nerve. Plus he was way too tired for swimming.

At 2:15 a.m. he found a phone booth on Doheny and dialed Adam Resnick's number. Adam told him that the cops were out looking for him and he needed to turn himself in. He told him that Fichman had negotiated with the DA, and that they would be lenient with him if he showed up at the Beverly Hills Hotel at four a.m. to give himself up. He also told Elliott that Gotti's people had talked with the family of the tourists who'd been nicked by the stray bullets, and that they said they didn't mind, they were just happy they got to meet a real-life semi-famous person—but unfortunately Rona Barrett was going to press charges. Gotti had offered the services of his high-powered attorney if Elliott would give himself up. Finally Resnick told Chris that *Get a Life* had gotten great reviews, with *Entertainment Weekly* calling it "the best new Fox show on Sunday between eight and nine, except of course for *In Living Color*."

"Okay. I'll turn myself in," Elliott told his friend. "I guess I got no choice. Thanks, Adam. I don't know what I would do without you. You're the best friend a guy could ever have." And then he hung up.

At 3:40 a.m., Chris staggered, bleary-eyed, into the Polo Lounge at the Beverly Hills Hotel and sauntered up to the bar. Laurence Taber, the bartender, was wiping a shot glass clean and remembers Chris looking disheveled and shaken.

"What, are you open or closed, Larry?" Chris asked.

"Always open for you, Mr. Elliott. Schnapps?"

"Make it a double."

Chris sipped his drink.

"Congratulations on the show, Mr. Elliott," Larry said. "I watched it. It's out there, that's for sure. The people I was with didn't get it, but *I* thought it was funny."

"Yeah, yeah, yeah. Show schmow. Who cares? My life's over. I took a potshot at Rona Barrett tonight. Now I gotta pay. That two-dollar hooker ain't gonna let me catch a break. I finally get my own show and I'm gonna be sent up the river. It's ironic, ain't it? After all these years in the business, the one thing I wanted—my own show—and now it's all going to be taken away from me. Oh well, they say I gotta turn myself in. Maybe it's the right thing to do. I've had a good ride. Don't you think, Larry? I've had a good ride, right? Larry?"

The moment Chris noticed that Larry was no longer there, a garrote was thrown around his neck from behind and pulled so tight that he began to choke.

"Help! Help, I can't breathe!"

"Andy Kaufman says hello," whispered a gruff voice in his ear, and then Elliott passed out.

TEN

Exactly what went down that night has remained a mystery to this day. The bartender, Laurence Taber, heard someone yell, "Freeze," followed by a bunch of loud pops. When he ran back out from the storeroom with a fresh bottle of schnapps, the police were already there and had already shot the assailant in the head.

The burly hood lay on the floor in a pool of crimson blood, and Chris lay on top of him, unconscious but still breathing, with a blissful expression on his face as though he were dreaming about something pleasant. (It's quite possible that the attack unwittingly triggered Elliott's sick obsession with autoerotic asphyxiation, which he later patented and tried unsuccessfully to market as a board game.) At any rate, he was rushed to Cedars-Sinai Medical Center, where he was revived, given a couple of aspirins, and then rushed to the Welcome

CHRIS ELLIOTT

Center at the LA County jail, where he was told in no uncertain terms to "wipe that fucking blissful look off your face."

"I want Andy Kaufman dead!" he fumed into a phone an hour later, sitting on one side of a dirty Plexiglas window, dressed in an orange jumpsuit.

"Pipe down. You gotta watch what you say in here," advised Bruce Cutler, the famous tough-as-nails Mob lawyer on the other side. "The bulls listen in on everything."

"Oh, I think that's a rather cynical view of the world, Mr. Cutler. I mean, *if* they were listening in, that would be tantamount to *eavesdropping*, *which I believe* is still a crime in this country if I remember correctly." Chris glanced over at a guard with a phone pressed to his ear. The guard grinned, winked, pointed at the receiver, and mouthed, "Yep, I can hear everything, asshole."

"Okay, just joking! Andy can live forever! He's great! He's the best in the whole wide world. I love him. He's a national treasure. He's the handsomest—the funniest—the—"

"Shut up," Cutler said. "Just relax. Everything's taken care of. You don't have to worry about Kaufman no more."

Apparently as soon as the boys at the Ravenite Social Club got word of the attempted hit on Elliott, Gotti put a hit out on Kaufman. Andy was so scared that he faked his own death (something he'd already done successfully back in 1984) and fled the country. Today, word on the street is that he is still alive, living comfortably somewhere in South America sipping daiquiris on a sandy beach and banging anything that isn't nailed down (to the sandy beach).

What Chris didn't realize at the time, however, is that it wasn't Andy Kaufman who tried to kill him. Sure he was the obvious choice, considering all the threats he had made on Elliott's life, but it turned out that those were just actual jokes. (Who knew?) The police suspected somebody else right away. "Andy Kaufman says hello" was just too obvious, after all. They saw it as a red herring. But if not Andy Kaufman, who else wanted Elliott dead? The list was, not surprisingly, a long one. The only clue was a card found inside the dead thug's jacket. It read, "Hello, my name is Jakunta. If you are reading this, then I am dead. Please remit my remains to Mr. Brando on Tetiaroa, and ask him to pack my ashes in a coconut and send them to my mother in Hasbrouck Heights. Also please save a lock of my hair and give it to my one true love, Bette Davis, with apologies for having failed her, because I'm assuming her idiot son is still alive if I'm dead. . . . Also thanks to my childhood mentor and math teacher, Mr. Levine—the one person who ever showed faith in me, and without whom I might have ended up a manservant to a much less talented actor on some smaller, crappier island—and finally a shout-out to Marsha Mason, my favorite Dorado, whose mutilated carcass rotting on the beach under the hot sun was a sight I shall never forget."

"When do I get out of here?" Chris asked.

"I'm working on it," Cutler replied. "It's complicated. Barrett's a tough broad. She wants a lot of shekels."

"Why? Is the exchange rate really good right now or something?"

Cutler paused, assessing the brain capacity of the guy he was dealing with, and shook his head. "Problem is, it ain't just her. They got you on attempted murder, racketeering, bribery, extortion, gambling, and fraud."

"What? Come on, that's crazy talk. I didn't do any of those things. I mean, *fraud*, yes. I've been a fraud all my life, although I don't know how they would have found out about *that*—unless Resnick sang!

That mother-grubber! When I get out of here I'll deal with that rat. I'll cut off his—"

"Shut up," Cutler barked. "They're just trying to intimidate you. They're not after you. They're after my man Johnny."

"Depp?"

"Um, no."

"Carson?"

"No."

"Angel? Quest? Reb?"

"No, what are you talking about? *Gotti!*"

"Mathis? Appleseed? On-the-Spot?"

"Just listen, will ya, kid—they want you to turn state's evidence and testify against him."

"Sure, I got no problem with that. Where do I get my belongings? Guard, be a dear and order me a cab—a nice sparkly yellow one, will ya? I'za go'n home, Momma. I'za go'n home!"

"Jesus Christ, shut the fuck up. Yes, you *do* have a problem with that."

"I do?"

"Of course you do! You can't rat out that man. Mr. Gotti's been your Godfather. You wouldn't have a career if it wasn't for him, and you definitely wouldn't have your own TV show. He's got Chernin by the balls—knows something about a dead weatherman found in the guy's hot tub or something."

Chris seemed sad. "Jeez, so I didn't get my show on my own merits, huh? It almost makes me feel like giving it back. *Almost.*"

"Kid, you couldn't get scabies on your own merits."

"Rub it in, why don't you?" A lump grew in Elliott's throat. "I guess I just wanted to be famous any way I could. But now look at me. I blew it. My career is over."

"Listen, kid." Cutler's voice became low and conspiratorial. "You got a lot of people on the outside working behind the scenes on the inside for you. That bitch Rona Barrett just wants to make you sweat a little. She'll settle. Trust me. Fichman is talking with the DA, Gotti plays golf with the judge, the President's on our side, as are most of the members of Congress, not to mention Lord Xenu, the grand dictator of the Galactic Confederacy, and as long I can get the money to the right people at Bob's Discount Furniture store, you got nothing to worry about."

It was at that moment that Chris realized Bruce Cutler was out of his mind.

"Uh-huh, *okay*," he condescended. "Whatever you say, Mr. Cutler."

The lawyer added, "Oh and by the way, I caught your show last night. Funny stuff. The people I was with didn't get it, but *I* thought it was funny."

Chris sighed.

"Just hang in there, kid, be strong. Give us a few hours here and I promise we'll get ya sprung." Then Cutler hung up the phone, and Chris made the crazy sign behind his back as he walked away.

Deloused, cuffed, and naked as a jaybird, Elliott was paraded down "new fish" alley, into "bugger me bum" corridor, and over to cell block three, also known as "the house of the rising piss-n-shit bag." Both tiers came alive as he passed, erupting in a cacophony of high-pitched catcalls. Cutler had requested that his client be held in protective custody, but the celebrity wing at the county jail was filled due to a SAG rally that had turned violent the day before when actor Viggo Mortensen took to the podium and—opting not to argue for increases in the pension plan—recited some of his dreadful poetry instead. So the best the judge could do was place Elliott in the women's house of detention for the time being. "He'll be safer there," the judge reasoned. "They'll just think he's an ugly chick with a beard— which is what I thought he was until somebody told me he was an ugly *guy* with a beard."

Elliott was dumped in a cell and handed a towel, soap, toothbrush, and a couple of tampons. The door slamming behind him lent an air of permanency to his predicament. He had just been through the longest and most trying day of his life, and he was emotionally and physically a wreck, not to mention half starved. He plopped down on his bunk and began to cry, then started munching on one of the tampons.

"Enough with the sniveling," a voice demanded from the top bunk, as two giant, filthy feet covered in thick calluses appeared about an inch away from Elliott's face. A moment later his celly hopped down with a grunt. Chris swallowed his tampon and gazed up in awe. The woman was about six feet tall and extremely broad-shouldered, with greasy, disheveled hair, blotchy red skin, and crazy eyes that drilled holes wherever they landed. Her crooked smile revealed a paucity of teeth, and gray exhaust billowed from her nostrils.

"How ya do'n, sweetcakes?" she said, extending her beefy hand and stomping her cigarette to death with her bare heel. "Name's Aileen. Aileen Wuornos."

Up to this point, Elliott had become adept at navigating the sexual loop-to-loops in the vast cosmos of Hollywood starlets, but in all his illicit assignations, his one true love had remained constant: Sweet Paula. She was his rock, the mother of his children, the woman who stood by him through thick and thin, who forgave his transgressions because she understood that just as great men have great flaws, stupid men have stupid flaws, too. But if Elliott's sex life was a roller coaster, he was about to get stuck upside down on the sexual equivalent of the Hell Loop 2000.

Aileen Wuornos's youth was marked by domestic violence, incest, and neglect, and by the time she was an adult she had been in and out of prison on various charges ranging from petty theft and vandalism to drug possession, prostitution, castration, and murder. Plus she was nuts. She was currently awaiting sentencing on charges stemming from a 1989 sting operation that nabbed her trying to sell counterfeit shoulder pads to an undercover fashion designer—a serious crime back in the eighties.

"Nice to meet you. I'm Chris. I love your taste in . . . blotchy skin and toothless . . . ness. And what, may I ask—if it's not too personal and won't piss you off—are you in the pokey for?"

Wuornos turned her head, hocked up a loogie, and gave it a powerful launch. It ricocheted off the walls, through the bars of the cell, and out into the common area where it hit a guard in the head, knocking him off his feet. "Damn you, Wuornos," the guard shouted, shaking his fist. "That's no Jell-O for a month! How you like that?"

Wuornos shouted back, "Eat me, you lousy, stink'n screw!" Then to Chris she said, "This time I'm in for shoulder pads, but I've been in and out of the slammer all my life, on account of society not getting my unique philosophy that the fucking male race is a blight on humanity. The sooner it's eradicated the better—hell, eradication is probably too lofty an idea, right? I'll settle for castrating 'em all. That's my goal in life. Wacka wacka wacka. What did you say your name was again?"

"Ah . . . Chris*tina*," said Chris in an even higher-pitched voice than usual.

Wuornos hugged him in her leathery armpit. "Well, I think you and me are going to be great friends. Let me know if my snoring bothers you."

"Sure. Right." Chris's eyes were beginning to water from the pungent fumes emanating from his cell mate, and also because he was already crying. "But my lawyer is going to get me out in an hour or so, so I wouldn't get too attached if I were you . . . ahahaha . . . I'd hate to see your feelings hurt."

But it turned out that Cutler had miscalculated, and it was going to take a little longer to spring Elliott. Hours dragged into days, and while his team worked to secure his release on the outside, Chris fell under Wuornos's irresistible spell on the inside.*

The two quickly became inseparable, which didn't take long, seeing as how they were locked up twenty-three hours a day. Wuornos started off by showing him the ropes. She taught him how to make "Pruno" (jailhouse hooch) out of mashed oranges, water, and sugar; and "Bligho" (jailhouse halva) out of mattress stuffing and shredded toilet paper (which, coincidentally, is exactly how they make it on the outside). She taught him who to associate with and who to stay away from, like the "Booty Bandits" in cell block C and the "Fanny Felchers" in the laundry room, who could all make easy prey of someone like Elliott were it not for Wuornos's protection. The two tried to stave off

---

* A nice way of saying he became her bitch.

insanity—which in both their cases was like a fish trying to keep dry—by staying busy. They played chess together, showered together, and perfected their own practice of yoga together, chanting à la *Midnight Express*, "Prison, monastery, cloister, cave, trailer park. Prison, monastery, cloister, cave, trailer park."

Late at night, Chris found himself rapt by Aileen's mindless ramblings. He gleaned deep meaning from the insane doctrines that she spewed from her top bunk.

"The world is a big garbage heap," she mused, as Chris feverishly wrote down her every word. "I never got nothing from nobody, and I ain't gonna give up nothing either, that's the way it works, nothing for nothing equals nothing. Get it? I'll fuck 'em all up, one of these days—fuck 'em all up. You get what I'm saying?"

"I sure do, honey. You hit the nail right on the proverbial head with that one."

Years later, on *The Mike Douglas Show*, Chris recalled with not a small amount of embarrassment the moment he succumbed to Aileen's enticing charms.

"She had a little tattoo at the top of her back," he told Douglas's audience. "And she was so tall you had to climb up a ladder to see it, and then you needed a spyglass to read what it said. I climbed up the ladder and looked in the spyglass, and it said, 'Fuck off, asshole!' I was so relieved. If it had said something negative like 'Ha ha—rip-off,' 'Joke's on you,' or something like that, then it wouldn't have meant anything, but it was so positive. I was immediately captivated. No pun intended, Mike, ha ha ha—no, seriously, I thought she was going to eat me."

But soon word came down that he was going to be released. After two weeks of haggling, Rona Barrett had finally agreed to settle—

with one caveat: She would drop all charges if Elliott would appear before a district court judge and in a public hearing answer under oath one or two simple questions put to him by the prosecution. It would not be a trial, *per se*—simply a hearing to clear the air. Fichman and Resnick thought it might be a good opportunity for Elliott to polish up his somewhat tarnished image, but they were dubious about Barrett's participation and worried she might have something up her sleeve. Cutler assured everyone that it was a standard legal procedure and would be quick and painless. "The fix," as he put it, "was in." So Elliott agreed to the terms and the televised hearing was set for November 1, 1990, at the Central District courthouse in downtown Los Angeles.

The room was filled with Chris's fans, his posse, the press, and John Gotti and his crew. Elliott entered looking sharp as ever in a conservatively cut gray suit lined with pink satin. On his head, for the first time ever, he was wearing a hairpiece. It was a convincing one (although he never had curly hair before), but it had been made from hair donated by somebody who'd died from an unfortunate medical condition known as seborrheic dermatitis, or "smelly-hair syndrome," so it gave off a repulsive odor no matter how many times it was washed.

"Mr. Elliott, would you please comment on your association with John Gotti?" the prosecutor asked right off the bat, making a point of holding his nose as he paced back and forth in front of Elliott.

"No. I would not," Chris answered, leaning back in his chair with a smug look on his face before winking at Gotti, who winked right back. "I got no association with the man. Don't know him."

"You deny that you even *know* John Gotti, the man sitting in the back of the courtroom wearing a 'Free Chrissy' button on his lapel?"

"I deny it, sir. And I resent the implication."

"Well then, could you please explain this photo?" The prosecutor held up a photo of a smiling Chris and John Gotti arm in arm surrounded by a bunch of kids at a Chuck E. Cheese's. They were all wearing party hats and holding noisemakers.

"You know, I take a hundred pictures with fans," Chris said. "That day, somebody said would you take a picture with my niece here, and I said sure, and before I knew it I was surrounded by a bunch of people that I did not know. That's all I can tell you about that."

"Sir, are you saying that you do not know *any* of the people in this photo?"

"I do not."

"Well, two of them are your children."

"Objection, Your Honor!" Cutler barked. "There's no reason to involve Mr. Elliott's family in this."

"Sustained. Move on to the next question," instructed the judge (and Gotti's golfing partner).

"Yes, Your Honor," said the prosecutor. "We really only have one other question for Mr. Elliott, and this one comes to us directly from Ms. Barrett herself."

He gestured toward the gallery, where Rona Barrett was already standing, holding a microphone. "Mr. Elliott," she said, "would you, here and now, on live television, and under oath, like to finally explain exactly what happened to you on Marlon Brando's private island?"

A loud murmur erupted in the courtroom. The judge banged his gavel and called for order. Elliott was obviously shaken by the question. His face went ashen. He wore the same expression that President Clinton had when he was asked about the cigar.

Cutler exploded, "I object, Your Honor! Whatever happened on that island, however long ago and however humiliating for Mr. Elliott, and however amusing it would be to hear it recounted in these proceedings at this moment, has no bearing here. This is just an attempt on Ms. Barrett's part to embarrass my client."

"I got no memory of that, Your Honor," Chris said. "I got no memory of it."

"You have no memory?" the smarmy prosecutor pushed. "That seems surprising, Mr. Elliott. No memory at all?"

"Okay, I think that's quite enough," the judge interrupted. "We needn't go into this matter any further. If there are no more questions, then this court renders Rona Barrett's complaint fully adjudicated and dismisses all charges against Mr. Elliott and thanks him for all the laughs he's given us throughout the years." Then the judge covered the microphone with his hand and addressed Chris directly. "By the way, I caught your show the other night. No one else in the room seemed to get it, but *I* thought it was really funny. Case dismissed."

A loud cheer went up from all those present. Barrett's scheme to get Chris to finally admit to what had happened on the island so many years ago had backfired, and the once powerful gossip columnist skulked back to New York City and into obscurity, while Elliott came out of the hearing smelling like a rose—and also smelling like a guy who had just spent two weeks having prison sex with a disgusting maniac before donning a hairpiece donated by a cadaver who basically stank himself to death.

Outside the courtroom everybody congratulated Chris.

"Hey, you popped your cherry!" Gotti said jubilantly as he threw his arms around Elliott.

"I thought you'd be mad at me," Chris said.

"How could I be mad at you?" Gotti replied. "You kept your mouth shut. That's the most important ting. You didn't tell 'em nut'n. I'm proud of yooz." He pinched Elliott's cheek. "Don't ever tell anybody nut'n. That's the secret to life. In fact, if you ever write an autobiography, just make up a bunch of bullshit and rip off a lot of dialogue from famous movies. It'll be more interesting that way."

* * *

Over the course of the next year, Elliott attempted to rehabilitate his image by doing volunteer work for Victoria's Secret, Frederick's of Hollywood, and *Hustler* magazine, but the combination of his arrest, his prison dalliances, and his evasive testimony at the Barrett hearing had sullied his reputation. The public was starting to sour on his bad-boy antics, and his fans were becoming increasingly uncomfortable with his off-screen womanizing, as well as with his ties to the Mob. In addition, he was psychologically traumatized from the whole prison experience, which only compounded all the other traumatic experiences that had been basically going on nonstop since childhood, and though he returned to the *Get a Life* set ready to work, he had become lackadaisical about the project. He refused to shoot any scene that required him to memorize more than three lines, and the morose side of his personality prompted him to demand that each episode end with his head being torn off and kicked down the street. "That's how my life is going to end anyway, right?" he would say. The writers were more than happy to oblige him because it meant that they didn't have to stay up late trying to write smart, funny closing jokes. (Or was ripping his head off and kicking it down the street smart and funny because it was so stupid?) The shows became increasingly surreal, not to mention controversial. For example, they did an episode in which Chris befriends a foul alien that spews gunk all over the place, which of course offended LA's growing alien community; they did an episode in which Chris travels back in time and through a series of high jinks accidentally becomes Hitler, which raised the inevitable objections from several major historical societies when he got the costume wrong—apparently the armband is always worn on the left? Consequently, the ratings began to slip, and Elliott, in permanent self-defeating mode, made little effort to save his own show, and so like any long-running TV series (*Get a Life* had only been on the air for about a season and a half, but *like* any long-running series), the show fell victim to its own desperate attempts to stay fresh, even going so far as to concoct a romance between Dame Robin Riker's character and Chris's—her sworn adversary. It was the same way *M*A*S*H* jumped the shark when Hawkeye and Hot Lips became lovers. (Or then again, maybe *Get a Life* was secretly being smart by making fun of *M*A*S*H*? Oh, who knows? And who gives a fuck, really?) All I know is that when a show loses sight of what it was originally, the writing is always on the wall, and in *Get a Life*'s case it had been on the wall from the start. In fact, Chris had to pass that very wall every day on his way into the studio. It got to the point where he didn't bother reading the sign anymore: "You're gonna get canceled—maybe even today, ha ha!" It was just something he had learned to live with, especially during the last month or so when the writing on the wall seemed extra big.

This was actually thanks to another classic Elliott misstep: early on, Chris had humiliated a junior executive in the promotional department at Fox by making ruthless fun of the man's ideas for *Get a Life* promos. He wanted footage of Chris running around *à la* the Keystone Kops with Benny Hill music playing in the background, an idea which had so offended Elliott's tastes that he resorted to yawning and making fart noises as the hapless executive desperately tap-danced in front of him. But halfway through *Get a Life's* run, there was a shake-up at the network that resulted in Peter Chernin, the show's original champion, moving on to higher ground and the lowly promo guy being promoted to Chernin's position in charge of all current programming. Now, not only was the writing on the wall—it was on the floor, the ceiling, and all over the bathroom mirror.

The ax finally fell on March 3, 1992, when not surprisingly Fox opted not to renew *Get a Life* for another season. Adam and Chris immediately tried to launch a number of other projects, including a cable movie version of their Steiner *Miracle Worker*, but nothing seemed to catch fire. They were about to give up when—at a charity event honoring Elliott—they received a cryptic proposal that would once again change their lives.

The night was April 1, 1992. Resnick had accompanied Chris to the Magic Castle on Franklin Avenue in Hollywood, where the American Association of Magicians, recognizing Elliott's outstanding contribution to the Families of Dead Escape Artists, was presenting him with a lifetime achievement award.*

---

* Okay, maybe not the most well-known charity in the world, but a worthwhile one nonetheless. Apparently, escape artists don't always make it out of their submerged trunks—at least one every twenty-five years gets stuck—and that man's family needs to be taken care of, damn it!

The Magic Castle was and still is a famous private club for magicians. The structure itself is a dramatic French château built around 1900, and is complete with a tower and a moat, and rumors of secret underground vaults and chambers. It's also full of antique artifacts from the bygone days of magic, like Harry Houdini's handcuffs, Ballantine's top hat, and Doug Henning's deodorant, which apparently had never been used. Various confounding "tricks" are built into the interior of the club itself, like moving bookcases, a player piano that takes requests, and a mounted bass that magically sings "Take Me to the River" whenever anybody passes by.

After the ceremony, Chris sat dejectedly beside Adam in the David Copperfield library. He tossed his lifetime achievement award into the fireplace and took a swig of brandy, which spilled down the front of his shirt. "Dribble glass. Very funny, Magic Castle."

"Yeah, comedy with a capital C," Adam added, equally down in the dumps. "We gave it a hell of a run, didn't we?"

"It's my fault, kid," Chris said. "I shouldn't have made fun of that guy's promo ideas. Stupid, stupid, stupid!" and he pounded his head against the wall. "Also I probably shouldn't have mocked everyone who tried to help me, or murdered all those innocent people."

"Nah. It's just the way things work," Adam replied. "Something else will come along. We'll get back on our feet before you know it."

The harsh reality of show business was starting to sink in. The dreams the two had shared back at Rudolf Steiner had come true, but now just as quickly the success that they'd worked so hard to achieve was slipping away.

"What happens now, Addy?" Chris asked. "I mean, what could we possibly do to top *Get a Life*?"

Just then there was a puff of smoke and a strange man wearing a tuxedo and a mask materialized in the library. Without saying a word, he handed Chris a card and dematerialized. On its own, this was not anything special. It was the sort of thing that happened all the time at the Magic Castle. It was even how you validated your parking. But then Chris opened the card and read the message inside: "You have been granted an audience with the Ghoul. Go to the bookcase and say the magic password."

More Magic Castle silliness, the two thought, but they walked over to the bookcase just the same. They waited, dumbly staring at the rows of books, but nothing happened. Suddenly there was another puff of smoke and the man in the mask reappeared. He seemed slightly annoyed at being back.

"Jesus Christ, what do you *think* the password is, guys?" Adam and Chris just shrugged. The mysterious man sighed, and mumbled, "We got a couple of winners here," then he turned to the books and exclaimed, "*Open sesame*, for God's sakes!"

The bookcase suddenly slid to the side, revealing a dark passageway. The masked man egged them on, "Go in, go in! The Ghoul is waiting for you." There was a torch mounted just inside the entrance. Chris took it and the two tentatively proceeded inside.

They descended a narrow stone stairwell. At the bottom they found themselves in what appeared to be a confluence of ancient catacombs. Spooky Danny Elfman music was piped in as they made their way through a short labyrinth of damp corridors, which ended at an enormous iron door. Standing in front of the door was the man in the mask and tuxedo again. "Your invitation, please."

"Hey, pal, it's us. You just saw us upstairs," Chris explained.

"Yeah, I know, but I need your invite. Otherwise you can't come in."

Adam and Chris searched their pockets.

"What did you do with the invite?" Elliott asked Resnick.

"I don't have it," Resnick said.

"You have to have it, because I don't have it."

"He gave it to *you*, not me."

"Well, I didn't know I was supposed to save it!"

"Oh, forget it," huffed the exasperated man in the mask. "Just follow me." He opened the door and they all entered what appeared to be a classic dungeon, complete with a rack, torches, and hanging cages. The man in the mask went over to the iron maiden in the corner and knocked three times, pulled out a set of keys and unlocked the lock. He opened it up and a figure stepped out dressed in a red skin-tight full-body latex suit with a chain around its neck and a ball in its mouth. Adam and Chris shared a confused look. Even by Magic Castle standards, this was a little kinky.

"Is that the Ghoul?" Chris asked.

"No, idiot. This is the *Gump*,"* the masked man replied. "The Ghoul is waiting for you in the other room. You present the Gump to the Ghoul when you see him."

"*What?*" Resnick was clearly ready to leave. "Come on, Chris, let's get out of here. This is too weird for me."

---

* Actually, it was just your standard-issue gimp, but my lawyers just informed me that Quentin Tarantino has recently trademarked the term for his extensive line of gimp-wear and gimp-themed skincare products, so even though this is a serious work of nonfiction, I apparently have to refer to it as a "gump." Sorry for the inconvenience.

"Wait. Not yet," Chris said. "We've come this far, let's see it through."

"All we did was walk down a set of stairs."

"Look, I know it's weird, Addy, but I feel like something wonderful is going to happen to us tonight."

"What can I tell you?" said the man in the mask. "It's all part of the stupid ritual or something. I just work here," and he handed Chris the chain attached to the Gump's neck. "Just give the Gump to the Ghoul. It'll make him happy. He's waiting for you in there." He pointed to another tall door and then disappeared with another puff of smoke, after which Chris observed, "My, but how people come and go so quickly around here," and he giggled.

The door slowly creaked open and Elliott and Resnick (with Gump in tow) entered a big ballroom that was dimly lit by candles. A handful of naked Amazonian women wearing carnival masks and stiletto heels stood around like mindless harem girls, and there was strange chanting going on somewhere in the background. A naked Amazon slowly approached the three of them and pointed to the center of the room. As they stepped forward, the throng parted, revealing a man in a red robe, black tights, and beat-up motorcycle boots. He was seated on a gold throne on a platform. His face was obscured by a cheap *Phantom of the Opera* mask, which only partially hid the expensive black sunglasses he was wearing underneath. In his hand he was holding a long staff topped with a silver skull. He stamped the staff three times, and the chanting stopped.

"Listen to the children of the night," said the king of this bizarre, erotic Comic-Con. "What beautiful music they make!"

"I don't hear anything," Chris observed.

The man sighed and stamped his staff again. "You must listen to the CHILDREN OF THE NIGHT!" At that point a scratchy recording of wolves howling echoed in the room.

"Oh right, yeah sure, now I hear them. Boy, that's great music, I really dig that rhythm, man."

"Have you brought me the Gump?" the man asked.

"Ah, yeah, sure, here he . . . er . . . she . . . er . . . *it* is—whatever." Chris handed the end of the chain to the man on the throne. The Gump immediately sat on the floor and retrieved a steno pad to take notes.

"Good. Then let's get down to business," the phantom said. "Ladies, hit the lights, would you, please?"

The room was illuminated and now Elliott and Resnick could see that they weren't in a ballroom at all, but rather a large office complex decorated with plastic skeletons, fake ghosts, grim reapers, and a bunch of rubber masks. It could have been the Halloween store at the mall were it not for the plethora of hip, young Hollywood types sitting at desks alongside animators at drawing boards and a handful of eager interns copying scripts at xerox machines.

The phantom laughed. "How do you like my production office?" he said. "It's reeeeeally creeeeeepy, wouldn't you agree?" Then he stood and ushered them into a smaller office, which was decorated in the more standard, scummy, Hollywood-executive style.

"I apologize for the theatrics employed in getting you here," he said. "But you see, I just can't resist a good spoooook! Brooooaha-hahahah. I hope you weren't too frightened." He removed his *Phantom of the Opera* mask, and Chris and Adam recognized him right away. The crazy black hair and designer sunglasses were the dead giveaway.

Tim Burton was the "it" kid in Hollywood at the time. He was, in fact, a product of Hollywood. Grown in a vat in Burbank and raised in the dungeons of the Magic Castle, Burton later attended the California Institute for the Arts, where he developed his own unique style of drawing, which exhibited a decidedly ghoulish flair (and wasn't at all a rip-off of Edward Gorey's work, or the entire nineteenth century). Burton first made a name for himself directing *Pee-Wee's Big Adventure*, and then went on to successfully incorporate his talents as an illustrator into other movies—like *Batman*, *Beetlejuice*, and *Edward Scissorhands*. Just like his contemporary Thomas Kinkade, the painter of light, Tim Burton—the painter of dark—had found a way to make art commercial, and now he wanted to piggyback on some of Elliott's and Resnick's magic.

"I'm a huge *Get a Life* fan," he said. "So sorry to hear it was canceled. What you guys do is reeeeally out there. Nobody else seems to get it, but *I* think it's funny. How 'bout we do a movie together?"

"Sounds good to us," Chris replied, speaking for Adam, too.

"Do you have any ideas?" Burton asked, petting the Gump's head.

"How 'bout a sea adventure like *Captains Courageous*?" Chris proposed.

At that moment it was as if everything froze. No one in the office complex said a word. The wall clock stopped ticking and the Gump dropped its steno pad.

"Yeah, I don't know . . . maybe," Burton grumbled, and tapped his desk methodically with his long, ghoulishly black-painted fingernails.

Adam and Chris looked at each other. They couldn't blow this opportunity. The time was now. They needed a new project—and a Tim Burton movie seemed just right. Somehow they would have to make this work. Then, as if the Magic Castle itself had sprinkled fairy dust over both of them, they came up with the same idea at the same time—and together they blurted out, "With creatures!"

Suddenly Burton perked up. They knew they had him hooked. "It'll be like *Captains Courageous* but with scary creatures!" Chris reiterated.

The Gump started scribbling feverishly again, the clock started ticking, and everyone went back to work in the big room.

It was no secret that Tim Burton had a soft spot for creatures, especially of the Ray Harryhausen/*Sindbad* type, and although Resnick and Elliott's instincts would have been to do a straight parody of *Captains Courageous* with Chris lost at sea with a bunch of burly sailors—along the lines of the popular construction worker episode of *Get a Life*, which Resnick had penned a year earlier—they knew that they would have to find something to appeal to Burton's insatiable fetish for all things "weird."

"That's it. Love it!" Burton exclaimed, jumping to his feet and inadvertently pulling the chain taut around the Gump's neck, causing it to let out a pathetic little whimper.

"It's . . . it's . . . it's . . . it's . . . it's exactly what I've been looking for. *A Pee-Wee's Big Adventure* for the nineties. I can see it now—weird and dark and creeeeeepy. A real brooooooding kind of comedy. Broooohahahahaha! What are we going to call this movie, boys?"

"Ah . . . call it? Um . . . ah . . . um." Again Adam and Chris looked at each other, and again the same thought hit them both like a lightning bolt: *"Cabin Girls Gone Wild!"*

"Love it!" shouted the Ghoul. "Let's go make movie history!"

"Wait just a goddamn minute," interrupted a strange and gruff voice behind them. "Anything sweetcakes does has to go through me first, understand?"

Everyone gasped when they saw who was standing there.

"Aileen! Sweetums," Chris said, wetting his pants, "you're out of the slammer—yay."

ELEVEN

On paper it looked like a guaranteed hit: the writing caliber of Elliott and Resnick, two of the most innovative voices in comedy, combined with the visual genius of Tim Burton, a proven commercial commodity, and the raw talents of Aileen Wuornos, one of the most prolific serial killers of all time. Jeffrey Katzenberg, head of the motion picture division at Disney from 1984 to 1994, and a lifelong fan of Chris Elliott's, was ecstatic when Burton brought him the package. Every other major motion picture company in Hollywood was vying for it, but Katzenberg's boundless enthusiasm had won Burton over. "When I first heard the idea, I flipped," Katzenberg told Walter Winchell at the film's premiere in Cannes. "I mean, come on, if somebody came up to you and said they needed thirty million to do a movie starring Chris Elliott lost at sea with a bunch of fat fishermen and a giant tobacco-spewing cupcake, wouldn't you flip, too?" But in retrospect he may have had ulterior motives. Tim Burton's "first look" deal at Disney meant that he could take the film anywhere he wanted if they passed on it, and Katzenberg, whose true comedic tastes favored movies like *Ernest—Scared Stupid*, may have worried that his mad genius of a director would jump ship if he didn't sign off. He also may have been terrified—as everyone with testicles was—of Aileen Wuornos, who insisted on sitting in on all the development meetings.

In fact, Katzenberg had a more personal reason to be scared of Wuornos, as she'd apparently disrupted a private luncheon between himself and Michael Eisner, the head honcho of the Disney Empire. The story, true or not, has become the stuff of Hollywood legend. Apparently she burst into the commissary while the two executives were enjoying their blackened mahi-mahi, grabbed Katzenberg by the collar and threw him over the buffet table. She then proceeded to tell him in no uncertain terms that "Either you do *Cabin Girls Gone Wild* or else I'll stuff your scrawny little ass in a trunk, drive you out to some lonely cornfield somewhere, and blow your fucking balls off!" It was obvious that although a novice in Hollywood, she was already becoming adept at the subtle art of negotiation. However, she may have crossed the line when she pointed a finger at Eisner and snarled, "You ain't no Walt." Nevertheless, as a result of her intervention, the Resnick/Elliott/Burton project was quickly green-lit, and Adam and Chris set about pounding out the story beats for the script.

They decided the plot would follow Elliott's true-life experience as a cabin boy aboard the Carnival Cruise ship *The Lady Liberty*, on which he stowed away so many years ago after running away from

Grey Gardens because Lee Radziwill made fun of his weird forked penis . . . triggering deep psychic wounds left by his mannish and equally bearded mother's boiling of his most beloved pet lobster . . . wounds that hadn't healed despite some moderate success at the boarding school where he'd been sent to treat the resulting case of hysterical blindness (in case you forgot). But after that, the story would veer off into the surreal. Chris's character would do battle with a whole host of mythical creatures, including Calli, an eight-armed seductress, and Chocki, a half man, half shark. Since the plot would revolve primarily around Elliott, and since there was no room for any bare-chested, inebriated college girls, they wisely changed the title to the more apropos *Cabin Boy*. Wuornos sat in the corner during these brainstorming sessions drinking beer and burping until she passed out, but occasionally she put in her two cents, and believe it or not a few of her ideas weren't so bad. For instance it was her suggestion that they change the name of the ship from *The Lady Liberty* to *The Filthy Whore* (a tribute to her mother), which Adam and Chris agreed added a bit of gritty realism to the script, but it was also Wuornos's suggestion that Chris speak in a bad English accent for no apparent reason—something that baffled both Elliott and Resnick as much as it did the reviewers. Fearing for their lives, the boys included most of her ideas, and it's quite possible that some of her off-the-wall touches helped make *Cabin Boy* the cult classic that it's become today. However, her insistence that she be given a major role in the movie was something Resnick and Elliott decided to let Tim Burton deal with when the casting process rolled around.

With the story in place, Adam went off to write the script, and Elliott spent the next month trying desperately to hide crazy Aileen from the prying eyes of Sweet Paula. It's unclear whether or not Sweet Paula suspected anything, but it's hard to imagine that she didn't notice Elliott leaving an extra plate of food in front of the attic door every night.

It's also highly unlikely that Sweet Paula never saw any of the stories appearing in the tabloids. The media dubbed Aileen Wuornos "the Dragon Lady" and portrayed her as a witch trying to drive a wedge between Chris and his wholesome wife. In truth, Elliott was trying desperately to find a way to ditch Aileen, but so far he hadn't been successful. He begged the boys from the Ravenite Social Club to whack her out, but even they were leery about messing with her.

Wuornos stuck to Chris like glue, and the press dogged their every move. In an attempt to shake them, she forced Elliott to sneak out of the country with her, but Al Capp, the wily *Li'l Abner* cartoonist, caught up with them at the Amsterdam Hilton, where twenty years after John Lennon and Yoko staged their famous bed-in for world peace, Wuornos and Elliott staged their own not-so-wholesome equivalent—this time for "world castration," a cause Wuornos had become increasingly passionate about, especially after spending so much time with Elliott.

With the newsreel cameras turning, Capp pulled up a chair and began to verbally berate "Mata Hari," as he called her.

"Look at you, you're a mess. You're disheveled, dirty, you don't look like a real lady. You should be wearing a pretty dress, and have your hair in a bow—and, sweetheart, maybe a little lipstick wouldn't hurt. And another thing, what's with all the four-letter words? Didn't your mommy teach you any manners?"

That was about all he got out before Wuornos jumped out of bed, wrestled him to the floor, and bit out his tongue. Luckily, Elliott had taken a heavy dose of Unisom and slept through the entire thing.

Back in the States, Wuornos insinuated herself into all aspects of Elliott's life, including his professional choices, and there seemed to be nothing he could do about it. She hired his services out to the Coyote Ugly Saloon, her favorite watering hole, where he was required to dance nightly on top of the bar wearing nothing but a cowboy hat, boots, and jockstrap (coincidentally, the same getup he wore when he played a tough, no-nonsense New York City cop in William Friedkin's *Cruising*). Irving Fichman's nose was out of joint over finding himself increasingly shut out, and although doctors installed the famous Jackson "tent" inside his septum, sadly it would remain out of joint for the rest of his life.

The press seized every opportunity to take potshots at Chris and the Dragon Lady. The last straw came when Gary Trudeau published a cartoon featuring Elliott—depicted as a fat cockroach—being pulled around on a leash by Wuornos—depicted as a giant flying vagina with teeth. Elliott tried to defend the relationship when he called into a local radio station.

"Before we met," he told Dennis Elsas of WNEW, "we were like two halves of one person. Well, I was smaller than a half—I was like a quarter, or even an eighth. Is an eighth bigger or smaller than a quarter? I never got the new math. Anyway, when we're together, we're like one big, ugly person—with a little extra plate of ugly on the side in case you're still hungry. No seriously, I'm afraid for my life. She's actually under the table right now holding a pair of gas-powered hedge clippers against my scrotum. For the love of God, send help."

But his babbling did little to sway public opinion. Unless something was done soon, he ran the risk of becoming cut off from those closest to him, including Sweet Paula (who luckily never listened to the radio), and also his yam bag.

*   *   *

"Love it!" Burton proclaimed, phoning Elliott and Resnick from his subterranean lair at the Magic Castle. He had just read Adam's first draft of *Cabin Boy*. "It's reeeeeally creeeeeepy and ghoooooulish, just the way I like my movies—and my women—and my hair—and my breath. It's perfect for me, but I'm afraid I'm not going to be able to direct it. I'm going to direct *Ed Wood*, instead."

"But who will direct, then?" Chris asked.

"Oh, I don't know . . . why not let Adam do it? It's not really that hard, basically you just run around the set saying a lot of creeeeepy and ghoooooulish things while a bunch of underpaid art and film students do ninety-nine percent of the work for you—yes, I want Adam Resnick to direct this wondrous thing called *Cabin Boy*. And it shall be so!"

Burton's sudden about-face was a shock, and not surprisingly Resnick was hesitant to shoulder the responsibility. Sure, he had directed a few remotes for *Late Night*, and of course the music video for Robin Byrd's memorable "Baby Won't You Bang My Box," but he had never given much thought to directing a feature. Elliott tried to convince his friend that it was the opportunity of a lifetime. "If the movie bombs," Chris told him, "no one will blame us, they'll blame Tim Burton." It was the same argument Sweet Paula had used to cajole Resnick into doing the Brando impersonation so many years before—and equally bullshit—yet somehow it worked. Adam agreed to direct.

Tim Burton would stay on as executive producer, and as such would "oversee all aspects of the production." Jeffrey Katzenberg's enthusiasm waned a bit when Burton opted out, so the budget was slashed from thirty million to a mere nine, and it now fell to first-time director Adam Resnick to shoot a special effects movie on a shoestring budget of about three million dollars—the remaining six going to Elliott's fee, and to pay for his various condiment addictions. Complicating matters, Burton took his highly skilled special effects artists with him to the *Ed Wood* project, so Resnick was forced to cull his team from the dregs of the industry; ironically, the only special effects guys available at the time were the same guys who did *Plan 9 from Outer Space*. But that may have been fortuitous after all. Now in their eighties, the team's shoddy workmanship only complemented the idiosyncratic charm of *Cabin Boy*, and the chintzy look of the special effects were one of the hallmarks (along with the incoherent plot, Elliott's perplexing characterization, and the bold absence of any genuine entertainment value) to which that one reviewer responded so favorably.

Shooting began March 1, 1993, and in a stroke of pure genius, Resnick cast Aileen Wuornos as the ice monster, which meant she would be encased in a giant cube of dry ice and kept in a deep freezer—conveniently out of Resnick and Elliott's hair—for most of the production.

The first scene to be shot saw Elliott as fancy lad Nathanial Mayweather, complete with Barry Lyndon wig and schoolboy shorts, prancing about his classroom in front of his bemused teacher—

played with a twinkle in his eye by actor extraordinaire Sir Alfred Molina, whose eye twinkle was less reflective of the joy he was experiencing playing the role and more likely an indication of how relieved he was to finally be getting his green card.

The rest of the cast was equally stellar: Russ Tamblyn as the half man, half shark, beautiful Ann Magnuson as the voluptuous temptress Calli, spunky Ricki Lake as the ship's Filthy Whore Figurehead, and Bob Elliott, the actor who eerily resembled an older Chris Elliott, returning once again to play Chris's dad.

Rounding off the players was David Letterman, reviving his "old salt" character from his days as a Down East storyteller for the pivotal role of "man who tries to sell Chris a sock monkey." Negotiations to nab him had been a legal nightmare. The main sticking point, contractually speaking, was that Dave didn't want to do it, but once that little snag was ironed out, Elliott braced himself for an uncomfortable reunion. They hadn't seen each other since Elliott quit *Late Night*, and as Chris remembered it, Dave had become extremely emotional when he heard that his favorite shoeshine boy was leaving. But Letterman was the consummate professional, and when he walked on the set he made sure to give Elliott a convivial greeting.

"Hey, how ya do'n there, buddy? Good to see ya." He embraced Chris in a tight bear hug, posing for photos and clowning for the visiting press. "You look great. Hey, remember when you used to come into my office with your little shoeshine box? Good Lord, I don't think anybody shined my wrestling shoes better than you did, pal." The crew and the boys in the press all laughed.

Chris was embarrassed, and his face showed it, but Dave didn't let up.

"I mean, this little guy here did the best spit and polish in the business. We called him 'Li'l Spit 'n Polish Elliott'!" Everybody laughed more, and steam began to blow out of Elliott's ears.

"Yeah, well, that was a long time ago," Chris grumbled, trying to contain his ire. "I'm the star of my own movie now, Dave. I don't shine shoes anymore."

"Oh, hey, I know that, buddy. You're a big celebrity now. Hey, I didn't mean anything by it. Congratulations on all your success, kid. I couldn't be happier for you. *Salud.*"

Chris narrowed his eyes suspiciously on Dave. "Okay. No problem," he finally countered, realizing he may have been overreacting. "No offense taken."

Letterman smiled. "Good. Glad to hear it." Then he took a swig of his Perrier and added, "Now go home and get your fucking shine box."

"Motherfucker!" Elliott jumped on top of his old boss, and the two started pounding away on each other. A bunch of burly grips had to break up the brawl.

But when the cameras rolled, any tension between Letterman and Elliott flew out the window, and they fell right back into the snappy repartee that was the benchmark of the chemistry they had shared for so many years.

DAVE (AS OLD SALT): Hey, you're one of them Fancy Lads, aren't cha?

CHRIS (AS NATHANIAL): Yes I am.

DAVE: Well, aren't you adorable. You're just the cutest little thing. You remind me of my sister. Would you like to buy a monkey?

Cabin Boy marked the first time David Letterman appeared on the big screen, and although it was brief, it was also quite powerful. As Pauline Kael of *The New Yorker* wrote:

> By injecting his old salt with scene-stealing vivacity the likes of which we haven't seen since the inimitable Huntz Hall, David Letterman makes a splash in *Cabin Boy*. If this is any indication of what's to come, then the *Late Night* host has a long and fruitful career in movies ahead of him, and we all have Chris Elliott to thank for being brave enough to take a chance on this talented newcomer.

The public was equally impressed, and the phrase "Would you like to buy a monkey?" immediately took its place alongside classic movie lines like "Let's blow this pop stand," "Who's that girl?" and "Slow down, man, I want to get there in one piece." According to Robert Osborne, who hosts a *Cabin Boy* marathon orgy every Halloween in his apartment, "Not only is 'Would you like to buy a monkey?' now one of the most beloved and oft-quoted motion picture catchphrases of all time, it's also the password to get into the orgy if anybody's interested. We could really use some more girls, frankly. . . ."

Elliott and Resnick were at their collaborative best during filming. Not since their days of melting cheese on lightbulbs had the two been so creatively unified. Indeed, the buzz surrounding the film was extremely positive, and industry insiders predicted it would be a huge hit. Before the movie was even finished, Elliott was already fielding offers for his next starring role, and although they didn't want to jinx anything, Adam and Chris both knew that after *Cabin Boy*, their careers would never be the same.

Still, Elliott may have been a little too confident. About a week before filming wrapped, Irving Fichman showed up at his trailer with a script in hand.

"Kid, it's time to pick your next movie. Take a look at this script. I think it's really funny, and the producers want *you* to be the star."

"Oh yeah? That's great, Irv," Chris muttered, callously fanning through the script. "But I plan on doing *Boy 2* and *3* after this, know what I mean?"

"Well, I know the vibe is good right now, but nobody can really predict what a movie will do. It's best to hedge our bets. How 'bout you look at the script for me, huh? If you like it, I'll call the producers and make the deal."

"Yeah, well . . ." Chris shifted in his chair and cleared his throat. "I've been meaning to talk to you about that, Irv. See, I think the situation being what it is, this might be a good time for us to make a change."

There was an awkward pause. Fichman couldn't believe what his good ear was hearing.

"What are you saying, kid? Are you firing me?"

"We're gonna make some changes, yeah."

"Kid, if it's something I did, tell me, and I'll fix it. I mean, we've been together too long. I can change. I can—"

"You're out, Irv."

Elliott's words hit Fichman like a sledgehammer. Regardless of whether or not Irv had seen it coming, there was no reason for Elliott to do it in such a cold and impersonal way.

"So the ship has already sailed?" Irv asked.

"That's right. The ship has sailed. I like that analogy. I've always been fond of the sea."

A faraway look crossed Fichman's face, as though he was remembering a gentler, more innocent time.

Chris pointed to the trailer door. "So, ah, thanks for everything, Irv, and don't let the door hit you in the ass on your way out. Just joking, but seriously, it's kind of my nap time, so . . ."

"I was just wondering . . ." Irving mused.

"Ugh. What now?"

"I was just wondering where that hungry, wide-eyed kid with the weak chin and uncontrollable drooling problem went. I just don't see him anymore."

"He grew up, Irv!" Elliott snapped back, getting in Fichman's face. "He grew up and learned how to play with the big boys. You're just a bloodsucking vampire! You said it yourself once! And I can't allow you to leach off me anymore. Times have changed, I need somebody who's with it—who's got their finger on the pulse—or at least *has* a pulse." Chris stopped. He knew he was going too far. "And right now," he continued in a more composed tone, "right now, I feel like the best choice to manage me is crazy, sweet Aileen Wuornos."

The old man began to deflate. "I see," he replied with a sad, broken voice, and his clothes seemed to get baggier and baggier as he continued deflating. "Well, I wish you luck. Don't worry about me. I'll be fine. I got lots of irons in the fire." He opened the trailer door. "But just do me a favor for old time's sake and take a quick look at that script. The boys who wrote it are hungry. Remember what it felt like to be hungry, kid?" Then he left.

Chris plopped back down on his sofa. He shot a look over at the script. "Stupid," he groused. "*Cabin Boy 2* is my next project. And then 3, 4, and 5, and then after that, I'm off to the toppermost, boys!" Again he glanced back at the script.

Maybe it wouldn't hurt just to take a quick look at the thing, he thought. *I guess I owe Irv that much.* He sighed, opened it up, and began to read.

He had barely gotten through page one before he snapped it shut and opened his trailer door.

"Listen, old man!" he shouted after Fichman. "Chris Elliott doesn't do lowbrow humor! You understand? Chris Elliott is the Noël Coward of his generation! Go tell your 'hungry' boys that this turkey doesn't have a snowball's chance in hell of ever being made!" And he flung the script out of his trailer and slammed the door.

Later that day, a young actor passed by and just happened to notice the script lying in the mud.

"Dumb and Dumber," he said. "Hmm, sounds positively delightful," and Jim Carrey stuck the script in his back pocket and skipped off to meet his agents for lunch.

* * *

As anyone in the film industry can attest, opening a movie is a delicate, choreographed ballet, combining complex elements of timing, publicity, and word of mouth. However, a film's success or failure often depends greatly on outside forces totally out of the control of the filmmakers. *Cabin Boy* received rave reviews, but the weekend it opened a record blizzard blanketed the East Coast, the Northridge earthquake rocked Los Angeles, and a bunch of twisters leveled most of the Midwest. It was also up against Pauly Shore's *Bio-Dome*, Kurt Russell's *Captain Ron* (another seagoing adventure), and Jeffrey Katzenberg's magnum opus, *Ernest Goes to Jail*. So when you take into consideration the effects of the stiff competition, and the fact that virtually every movie theater in the United States had been shut

193

down or destroyed, it's not surprising that *Cabin Boy* didn't fare well its first weekend at the box office. (Also there was a newspaper strike on, so the rave reviews never made it to print, plus an epidemic of laryngitis pretty much put the kibosh on the whole word-of-mouth thing.) Still, a few hearty, die-hard Chris Elliott fans braved the inclement weather on the East Coast, the riots on the West Coast, and the rubble littering America's heartland, and sought out the germ-proof underground cinemas where make-shift screens had been improvised. Those who got a chance to see the film that fateful weekend were treated to a rare, life-altering experience comparable to viewing *Fantasia* on acid (or reading this book, sober), and it's largely thanks to those brave underground souls that *Cabin Boy* became such a huge underground hit. At the time, however, the underground market wasn't big enough, and by Monday morning, all those who didn't identify as a mole-man had officially labeled the movie "a bomb."

Bette Davis's curse had reared its ugly head yet again. Elliott was devastated. It was like the Oriental carpet had just been pulled out from underneath him. His dream of an entertainment revolution that would forever alter who we laugh at and why had once again blown up in his face.

Burton and Katzenberg immediately distanced themselves from *Cabin Boy*, putting out a joint statement that simply read: "Don't blame us, we've never heard of the guy. In fact, we don't even speak English. *¿Qué pasa?* Who es dis Chris Elliott you saying?" Elliott's postulation that if the film failed it would be Tim Burton's cross to bear could not have been more misguided. Everyone blamed one person and one person only: Chris Elliott.

Aileen Wuornos, enraged that the big scene where the ice monster castrates the fisherman had been castrated from the film, embarked on a cross-country murder spree in which she targeted only bald, stupid guys with beards, shooting them in the groin and always leaving her "Personal Management" card sticking conspicuously out of their mouths.

The weekend *Cabin Boy* opened turned out to be one three-day-long nightmare for Elliott. Those seventy-two hours were the most painful, demoralizing, and humiliating of Elliott's entire life, next to the agonizing three days it always took to clean his teeth.

The news of Irving Fichman's death only added fuel to the conflagration of bad luck. Distraught over being fired, Irving had returned to New York City and to a coffin at the Belvedere Castle in Central Park. Apparently, he'd taken Elliott's words to heart—literally. They found him in a cheap Count Dracula costume with a wooden stake sticking out of his chest. Chris got the message loud and clear. He deeply regretted his argument with Irving, who in the end had been absolutely right—Elliott should have hedged his bets.

Thinking he could save his reputation by touting the populist line, Elliott jumped on board the "blame Chris Elliott bandwagon." He blamed himself for *Cabin Boy*, for Fichman's suicide, and for the bizarre sex tape that Wuornos and Elliott had made during their "bed-in," in which an inebriated Wuornos is seen performing a series of complicated "myth-busting" procedures on Elliott, who appears to be fast asleep. Right after *Cabin Boy* opened, and right before her murder spree, Wuornos had the good sense to drop the tape off at TMZ.

Adding insult to injury, Gay Talese's *Esquire* article, titled "Chris Elliott Has a Cold," hit the newsstand that same awful weekend.

The profile, considered by many to be one of the most in-depth and overwritten in history, was anything but complimentary. It described a sullen, middle-aged comic actor, with the sniffles, insecure about his looks and lack of talent, bar-hopping and skirt-chasing his way through a dark warren of Hollywood hot spots.

> The man stands at the bar in the dimly lit Hamburger Hamlet, his pink lizard lips osculating the rim of his glass as he reenacts love's first kiss, and then in a flash he summarily downs his tenth raspberry schnapps. The bartender knows his cue and quickly refills. The woman next to the man, faceless, hairless, and naked to her soul, whose only purpose is to light his Gitanes and satiate his hunger for a gobbet of cheesecake delivered directly to his open maw on her freakishly protracted tongue, has no reference for why the man is important. His contribution to the world of comedy is to her no more relevant than last month's copy of *People* magazine. Chris Elliott has a cold and he's in a bad mood. And perhaps he should be. He stands on the precipice of total demise. One false move—like if *Cabin Boy* bombs—and he could be sent over the edge into the abyss of yesterday's news. In fact, it is only by the charity of his few surviving fans, fatigued as they are by his special brand of comedy that professes to be funny only because it's not funny—which is such an obvious contradiction that frankly he really should have seen this coming—but softened by their collective memories of his past triumphs, that he's still allowed a seat at fame's table. But the fame restaurant is closing soon, and he'll have to find another place to be seen—or else he'll die—because his true addiction isn't schnapps, it's being moderately famous.

The profile went on to describe Elliott as a "boorish womanizer" and detailed a number of his illicit Hollywood liaisons. Sweet Paula, who had assumed the Wuornos sex tape was simply a practical joke and just laughed when she watched clips of it on *Entertainment Tonight*, was now shocked and enraged when she read about Chris's affairs. She had lived every day with blinders on, but after the *Esquire* article she had a revelation. She wasn't going to look the other way anymore. Sweet Paula had finally wised up.

So the same weekend that *Cabin Boy* opened and bombed turned out to be the very same weekend that Irving Fichman killed himself, and the same weekend that Aileen Wuornos released the sex tape to the media, and the same weekend that the *Esquire* article came out, *and*—on top of all that—the same weekend that Sweet Paula dumped Chris Elliott.*

* * *

It was all more than one man could take. Chris went plain off the deep end and into a dark depression, and an endless cycle of self-mutilation followed, which was followed in turn by a period of self-medication, which didn't do a thing for the self-mutilation (because it wasn't that sort of medication). For months he wandered the streets of LA, lost in a kaleidoscope of hazy memories, huddled against dumpsters, sucking on his tartar pipe and drinking schnapps nips out of tiny brown paper bags. He eschewed bathing, grooming, and eating; his expensive clothes rapidly became a raggedy man's wardrobe. At night he would shuffle past his old haunts, looking in the windows of the places where he once held court—places like the

---

* Determined never to be duped again, Sweet Paula took the twins with her and returned to the Bram in New York City and to the support of the one person she knew she could always trust, Ruth Gordon.

Daily Grill, Barney's Beanery, and El Pollo Loco, where the maître d's all knew his name. A new breed of young upstart talent now occupied his tables, and the maître d's closed the blinds so the young Turks wouldn't have to see the sad shadow in the window—a shadow that might one day engulf them. It was the old story—Hollywood was turning its back on one of its own yet again. And just when it seemed Chris Elliott could not have fallen any lower, he stopped shuffling about and started crawling, leaving a long trail of glistening shame behind him as he went.

He crawled his way out to the Pacific Palisades and camped out up in the hills of Temescal Canyon, where he found solace in the isolation. But it was there among the eucalyptus trees, wild bobcats, and occasional hobo looking for companionship or just a cup of Sterno, that he came face-to-face with his worst nightmare—himself.

It was an autumn night, and he was roasting a weenie on his campfire when he heard rustling in the bushes.

"Who's there?" he called out, cocking his Glock. "Is that you, Hobo Luke?"

"No, it's me. I've been looking all over for you," said Adam Resnick, stepping out of the brush.

"Adam, is that really you?" Chris couldn't believe his eyes. "But how did you find me?"

"It wasn't hard. I just followed the long trail of glistening shame."

Chris was happy to see his old best friend again. He broke out a fresh can of beans and whipped up a batch of jungle juice to mark the occasion. It had been a long time since *Cabin Boy* opened and closed, but the movie had driven a wedge between them. There was a lot of water under the bridge, and although the movie's failure had affected Adam as well, he hadn't given up on his own life or career as Elliott had. In fact, Resnick was already working on another screenplay, so there was much to catch up on. The two stayed up talking into the night, reminiscing about the past and becoming more and more intoxicated—to the point where they were finally able to laugh about the whole *Cabin Boy* experience, especially the part about Tim Burton wearing tights.

After a while, they became fatigued and lay on their backs looking up at the stars. Elliott began to wax nostalgic about the good old days at Rudolf Steiner.

"Oh, what I wouldn't give for another dance with Sally Jenkins," he mused.

Adam just grunted.

"I said, what I wouldn't give for another dance with Sally Jenkins."

"Yeah, sure, Sally Jenkins," Adam affirmed drowsily. "That math teacher we murdered, right? She sure was something."

Chris suddenly eyed his old friend suspiciously, closely inspecting the double lightning bolt tattoo on his arm. . . .

"It's getting late," Resnick mumbled. "Let's get some shut-eye. I got you an appointment with a new manager tomorrow. He's supposed to be very good. We still got a few tricks up our sleeve, kid." And then he dozed off.

But in the middle of the night, Resnick woke up with Elliott on top of him pointing his Glock in his face.

Adam gasped. "What the hell's going on?"

"I want you to tell me something," Chris commanded in a gravelly voice. "Who is Sally Jenkins?"

"What?"

"Who is Sally Jenkins?"

Adam hemmed and hawed for a moment.

"Okay, so not the teacher—right, sorry I was tired, before. She was, uh, a girl you had a crush on at school, right?"

"Um . . . okay, lucky guess. But what did she look like?"

"I don't know, she had braids, and wore big glasses?"

"Okay, another good guess. What kind of clothes did she like to wear?"

"She always dressed in black?"

"Oh, you're good. You're very good. But what size *shoe* did she wear?"

"What?"

"Answer me! What size shoe did she wear?" Sweat pellets appeared on Adam's forehead, and his mouth went dry.

"I can't remember."

"Aha! I knew it!"

"Knew what? *You* tell me what size shoe she wore."

"If you were the real Adam Resnick then you would know that I was always talking about how cute her little size-six Frankenstein boots were. Now who are you?" Elliott asked.

"Chris, come on, that was years ago."

"I said, who are you?" Chris cocked his gun and pushed the muzzle into Resnick's cheek. Resnick paused and took a deep breath.

"I'm no one, Chris. Just let me go and I'll never bother you again."

"Who is 'no one'? Tell me who the hell you really are and I'll let you go."

Adam, or whoever he was, tried to swallow, and his voice cracked as he spoke.

"Okay, it was the early eighties, I was drinking in a bar in Harrisburg, Pennsylvania. You were on the TV doing your Panicky Guy bit. Everybody was laughing. There was this giant sitting at the bar next to me. He had to be about twelve feet tall. He introduced himself as your old school buddy from Rudolf Steiner, Adam Resnick. He said it was his last night in the States because he was leaving in the morning for Russia to undergo some experimental treatment for his giantism. He told me all about himself, and all about you, Chris. He really loved you. The next day I took him to the airport, made sure he got on his plane, and then I applied for a writing job at *Late Night*. I pretended to be him. It turns out I'm kind of a brilliant comedy writer. I guess you don't have to go to Harvard for that shit, after all. But I'm your friend, Chris. I really didn't mean anything by it. I was just trying to make a buck and I thought I could help you in your career, and I think I have, right? We've been through so much together. Don't let *Cabin Boy* tear us apart, or, you know, the fact that I've lied to you for ten years."

The loud report of the gunshot shattered the night and echoed through the canyon.

Afterward, Elliott sat there in the dark, reflecting on the dismal state of affairs in which he now found himself. He was completely alone. His career was over. His longtime manager was dead. His wife had left him, and he had just killed the one person—impostor or not—who had stood beside him, the man who put the jokes in his mouth for all those years, the man whose sense of humor he trusted more than his own. Adam Resnick, the great fixer, was gone. There wasn't much left for Chris to do, except turn the Glock on himself, but he just didn't have the guts.

The next morning Elliott woke to the harsh glare of the sun shining directly into his eyes. The glare was extra harsh because it was glinting off the shiny badge of an LA police officer.

"You Chris Elliott?"

"Huh, what?" Elliott mumbled, and he rose up, resting one elbow on the freshly filled grave of the man he'd shot the night before. "What did you say?" he asked, shielding his eyes from the glare.

"Your name Chris Elliott?"

"Who wants to know?"

"Not me, fella," said the officer, wincing at Chris's body odor, which had been activated by the warm morning sun. "But this guy asked us to find you."

The cop stepped aside, revealing a tall, slim man with a neatly groomed beard, dressed entirely in black. He was doing tai chi, and he spoke rapidly, like he was on speed.

"If you wanted to cancel our meeting, I wish you would have called my assistant. I'm a very busy man. Anyway, your friend Resnick said you were looking for a new manager. I think I can help revive your career. Name's Polone. Gavin Polone."

He stopped doing tai chi for a second and produced a script almost magically from out of nowhere on his body. "Here, take a look at this. I had to pull a lot of strings, but I got you a meeting for three o'clock this afternoon. Oh, and here's a couple of bucks to clean yourself up." He threw a wad of cash at Elliott. "Don't be late." He did a full roundhouse air kick and started to leave. "Oh, and call my assistant afterwards to tell me how it went."

When Polone and the cop had disappeared back down the path, Elliott began to flip through the script.

"*There's Something About Mary,*" he said out loud. "Sounds positively enchanting . . . though I'm not sure this Dom character is *wretched* enough. I believe he needs some boils or something."

TWELVE

My recent work at the Karlstadt Institute for the Criminally Insane confirms my supposition that to truly comprehend the underlying psychosis exhibited by Chris Elliott, one must go beyond the accepted boundaries of x-ray computed tomography and magnetic resonance imaging, and into the realm of the operating room for a comprehensive dissection of the man's puny little brain, preferably while he is still alive, and minus anesthesia. Of course I could always just stab the *arschloch* in the chest while he's sleeping.

—DR. AMELIA ADLER

If we give you this role, we're not going to put up with any of your shenanigans, tomfoolery, or monkeyshines," warned Peter and Bobby Farrelly, the comic geniuses behind *Dumb and Dumber*, a movie that ended up being a huge box-office hit. "We're not joking here," they added simultaneously. The brothers were both of one mind and always spoke in unison. "We've heard the stories," they continued, as they stroked the frogs they held in their respective laps. "And quite frankly, we're appalled by some of your past behavior." Elliott's reputation had preceded him, and although he had been the Farrellys' first choice for the role of Dom Woganowski in *There's Something About Mary*, the brothers ran a tight ship, and they were leery about hiring such a notoriously erratic personality. "We're serious men," they stressed somberly, "and there's no room for any capers, stunts, escapades, or folderol of any kind on our sets." Then, to drive the point home, they dropped their pants and seriously mooned him. They knew "Woogie" could revive Elliott's career, and that Elliott wanted the role badly—so badly that he might say or do anything to get it. Chris tried to assuage their fears. "I understand your concerns," he said, "and I swear, gentlemen, if you give me the part, little Chrissy will be a good boy and mind his p's and q's." He stuck a thumb in his mouth and made a cute face. But Peter and Bobby were no pushovers—if Elliott really wanted the role, he was going to have to work harder than that. So Chris stripped down to his diaper, climbed into a crib, and began to cry like a baby. "Whaaaa! Chrissy wants to be in the movie! Chrissy wants to be in the movie. Whaaaa!" Despite Elliott's adorable cherubic charm, the Farrelly brothers were still on the fence, and just to make sure Elliott knew who was in charge, they stood up and wagged their serious schlongs in his face. (Apparently, it wasn't just frogs they had been stroking.)

It had been a struggle for Elliott just to get to this point. His name had come up early in the casting process, but his old friend Peter Chernin, now head of 20th Century–Fox, wanted Charlton Heston for the role. Heston was hot off his powerful portrayal of Lord Togrul in the ill-fated epic *Genghis Khan* and was being wooed by Jack Warner to play King Lianas P. Truffle-head III in the soon to be ill-fated epic *The Mushroom Chronicles, Episode One: Fungi Rebellion*. Chernin felt the *Planet of the Apes* actor would bring a sense of quiet nobility to the role of Dom Woganowski. He was also hesitant to hire Elliott knowing he'd probably murdered his actual mother on the set of *Get a Life*.

Elliott knew that *There's Something About Mary* could put him back on the map, so he pulled out all the stops campaigning for the role. He called his old friend Shelley Winters and begged her to use her extensive Hollywood connections to help him land it. Winters had a direct line to Chernin's ear. She was best friends with Elia Kazan's wife, Frances Rudge, who had lived next door to the Kenneth Galbraiths, whose housekeeper was Rosita Salazar, the sister of Gomez Salazar, the Chernins' pool boy, who got word to Chernin through an interpreter that in his opinion they needed a more concentrated algicide, especially in the hot tub where the local weatherman had been found dead . . . and *by the way* don't you think Chris Elliott would be perfect for the role of Dom Woganowski? But Peter Chernin wasn't about to just hand Elliott the part. Fox made Chris do a screen test, which was a huge humiliation for an actor of his caliber, not to mention a threat to his health. The last audition he'd gone on was for a job as a greeter at Walmart. He had become so nervous waiting with the other elderly women that he passed out and was given mouth-to-mouth resuscitation by a blue-haired octogenarian, which—had he been conscious—he probably would have enjoyed. So in an attempt to make it less stressful on him, the Farrellys arranged for the screen test to be shot in Elliott's trailer in Encino.

The brothers recalled the extraordinary day: "When we first arrived, Chris greeted us at the door in complete blackface. He explained that that's how he imagined the character of 'Dom—The Interlocutor.' When we informed him that *There's Something About*

Mary was a movie and not an old-time minstrel show, he seemed genuinely embarrassed. 'I'm so sorry, my mistake. I got another idea, hang on,' and he washed off the shoe polish, ran outside and rolled around in the bushes for about twenty minutes. We looked at each other like, 'What the hell have we gotten ourselves into with this guy?' but when he came back inside, his face slowly broke out in big red welts, because apparently he had been rolling around in poison ivy. At that moment we knew we had found our Dom Woganowski!"

Chernin had also been impressed when he saw the screen test and immediately signed off on Elliott, but the brothers were still afraid to fully commit because of Elliott's well-known history of mental, emotional, and digestive problems. (The latter having caused the Metamucil budget to skyrocket on his last three pictures.)

Over breakfast at the Four Seasons, Bruce Cutler stressed to the Farrellys how appreciative John Gotti would be if Elliott got the part, but they told Cutler that they hadn't made any firm decisions yet, and they weren't going to be swayed by any outside opinions. "We're dangerous men," they advised Cutler sternly. "Don't screw around with us." And then, just to drive the point home, they gave the tough lawyer a couple of seriously painful titty twisters. This didn't sit well with Cutler, who hadn't been titty-twisted since his initiation into the Gambino crew. After he left in a huff, the Farrellys discovered the severed heads of their pet frogs floating in their respective coffee cups. Apparently, Cutler had been decapitating the frogs with his penknife under the table during breakfast, but the brothers didn't make that connection. They just assumed it was a horrible freak accident, and blamed each other for forgetting to put the lid back on the frog jar and reprimanded the waiter for leaving the bagel cutter out on the table. Not until they stood up, however, did they realize that Cutler had been deftly cutting off something far more personal, and it tweren't frog heads. (The giveaway was the empty can of spray anesthetic lying on the floor.) They immediately got their coffees to go and scurried off to Cedars-Sinai Medical Center for emergency reattachment surgery.

"And you swear to us that you're clean?" they grilled Elliott one last time from the hospital bed they shared in the intensive care ward. "He's clean. I can attest to that," pronounced the voice of God—or the next best thing to God, at least in Hollywood: the voice of Dr. Drew Pinsky, the addiction specialist who had worked tirelessly to rid Elliott of his dependency on acetic acid and egg yolks— the active ingredients in street-grade tartar sauce. "Also, in my opinion," Pinsky added, throwing an arm around Elliott, "you should give my buddy here the part he wants, otherwise you might not get the 'parts' *you* want, if you know what I mean." Pinsky was heading up the medical team in charge of reattaching the Farrellys' "frogs," and so *his* opinion was the only one the brothers needed to make their final decision.

Filming began in the spring of 1997 in Providence, Rhode Island, and from the start it was obvious that Elliott was exhibiting a new side of his multifaceted personality. No longer relying on the old standby of being funny by not being funny, he was actually *acting* for the first time in his career, and his performance was nothing if not short of scintillating. He was truly born to play Dom Woganowski— ironically, a guy who was pretending to be somebody he wasn't.

It was a stripped-down Elliott who appeared on set bright-eyed and bushy-tailed and eager to do the work each day. He had lost about four hundred pounds and was no longer wearing the smelly hairpiece (which itself had weighed about forty pounds). He was professional and intense during shooting, determined to be seen as an actor on the same level as Brett Favre. Chris became close friends with his costars Ben Stiller and Matt Dillon, and the three often went out for steak dinners at McCormick & Schmick's or for all-night parties over at Mayor Vincent "Buddy" Cianci Jr.'s place. A controversy arose one night when Cianci caught the three of them in bed with his wife, and the mayor was forced to spend the next six months behind bars for assaulting the actors with his lit cigarette, but Ben, Matt, and Chris came out of the debacle smelling like roses.

There's Something About Mary was a huge hit, yet Elliott's portrayal of Dom Woganowski received mixed reviews. The bold choices he made were both provocative and divisive. His performance was singled out by *Variety* as being "stunning," while *The Hollywood Reporter* called it "lackluster." This split in public opinion only fueled curiosity in the film, and Dom Woganowski became the character audiences most readily identified Elliott with. For years afterward, he couldn't walk down the street without having somebody yell out, "Hey, Woogie" (at least until his face had finally cleared up).

Gavin Polone's phone started ringing off the hook with offers for his new client. It was the old story—Hollywood was rediscovering one of its own. Perhaps the classic "big comeback" had eluded Elliott, but the Farrelly brothers had given him something far more valuable. Even if the role had not been the career changer that he had hoped it would be, *Mary* positioned Elliott in that rare and coveted spot in show business, enjoyed by only a handful of atypical provocateurs, like Antonio Salieri, Carrot Top, and Yahoo Serious: "meaty okra" talent blessed with a constant stream of steady work.

Over the course of the next several years the offers kept rolling in. He did a number of television pilots, among them *Out There* for ABC, produced by Gavin Polone, about a grown-up paperboy who moves from the country to the big city, and *You've Reached the Elliotts* for CBS, about a grown-up paperboy who moves from the big city back to the country—but without Adam Resnick by his side he was never quite able to re-create the imbecilic charm of *Get a Life*. He did, however, do several imbecilic cameos in hit movies like *Scary Movie 2* and *Scary Movie 4*, and had recurring imbecilic roles on television shows like *Murphy Brown*, *The Naked Truth*, *The Webber Show*, *Everybody Loves Raymond*, *Under the Umbrella Tree*, and *Zoobilee Zoo*—2005.

As time went on, he stretched his wings as a performer, writer, and male prostitute. He was a jack-of-all-trades and a master of none, especially when it came to prostitution, which he had very little luck with. During this period, Gavin Polone cajoled Swifty Lazar, the high-powered literary agent who represented the likes of Cher, Madonna, and Ernest Hemingway, to take Elliott on as a client. Unfortunately, Lazar had no experience pimping male prostitutes, so he pushed Elliott's pathetic literary samples instead. He had to work hard just to get anyone to read the amateurish material that was always handwritten on napkins, but eventually he persuaded Bennett Cerf to publish Elliott's first book, entitled *Daddy's Boy: A Son's Shocking Account of Life with a Famous Father*. It was a memoir of sorts detailing Chris's life growing up in San Semolina as Sam Elliott's son. Oddly enough, he never once mentioned that his mother was a famous movie star (Bette Davis's daughter BD beat him to the punch with that one). As it turned out, Elliott didn't have much to complain about when it came to Sam Elliott, and *Daddy's Boy* was simply not salacious enough to be a bestseller—a mistake he would never make again.

A year later, Cerf published Elliott's *Into Hot Air*, a salacious adventure story chronicling his 2006 charity climb up Mount Everest with a bunch of celebrity pals, which had ended tragically—at least for Michael Moore, who lost several toes to frostbite, as well as several bags of frozen beef jerky somewhere up on the Hillary Tit. *Into Hot Air* was an immediate bestseller, as was Elliott's third book, *The Shroud of the Thwacker*, a salacious adventure story chronicling his attempts to solve the infamous "Thwacker murders" that plagued New York City back in the late 1800s. His solution was as controversial as it was idiotic—he claimed to actually be the Thwacker killer himself, and that he had been time-traveling back and forth through a portal in the planetarium at the Museum of Natural History. Although his fans hailed both books as works of "comic genius," Elliott had never meant either of them to be funny, which most reviewers understood (or at least they understood that they weren't funny). Elliott was incensed that the literary community would not take his work seriously, but the truth was that even after all these years, he was more deluded than ever. All the great absorber had done was simply absorb, or rather rip off, Jon Krakauer's *Into Thin Air* and Caleb Carr's *The Alienist*, but he truly believed he had climbed Mount Everest with Michael Moore and Tony Danza, and that he really was the reincarnated nineteenth-century serial killer who dispatched his victims by thwacking them upside their heads with a sack of McIntosh apples.

But the more adamant Elliott was about the veracity of his books, the more popular the books became, because everyone just assumed it was all part of his act. Even at this point in his career, his audience was still mistaking his innate ham-headedness for calculated stupidity.

He continued to work steadily on and off screen for the better part of the next decade, but the jobs he chose were, for the most part, "under the radar"—nothing particularly high profile. He invested in a number of side ventures that went belly-up, including his manscaping company, which was shut down because he was employing illegals to do the chest hair trimming, but as far as the entertainment world was concerned, the real Chris Elliott was gone—absorbed into the slow-moving caramel sludge of mainstream schlock.

As his voice melded into the background noise of middle-of-the-road American humor, a new breed of funny people began to surface, and Elliott couldn't help but sense the menacing shadow of age creeping up behind him. David Letterman moved over to CBS and was replaced at NBC by Conan O'Brien, the young upstart, who picked up the torch and effortlessly pushed the envelope even further than his predecessor had, and who was then in turn replaced by the even younger, more envelope-pushing upstart named Jimmy Fallon. In movies, the Judd Apatow force of nature eclipsed the Farrelly brothers' reign, and new faces like Steve Carell, Seth Rogen, and Will Ferrell relieved the old guard formerly under the command of Robin Williams, Jim Carrey, and Yakov Smirnoff, and eventually the great Sacha Baron Cohen took Andy Kaufman's place as the king of all avant-garde comedy.

With the explosion of cable television, a new comic revolution led by brilliant writer/performers like David Cross, Bob Odenkirk, and Sarah Silverman, and anybody who had ever signed up for a class at UCB, took the nation by storm, and with the advent of the Internet, aspiring comedians with virtually no experience whatsoever could now expose themselves to a huge audience, simply by beating off in front of their iPhones (thank you, Steve Jobs—lovely legacy). Unlike the old days, when *Late Night* and *Saturday Night Live* were the only venues to explore comedic boundaries, now, thanks to YouTube, Twitter, and Funny or Die, millions of new voices found blank canvas on which to experiment, and the comedy community seemed more interconnected than ever before. Everyone knew everyone and the line between audience and performer slowly evaporated, until it became difficult to tell the novice from the real deal, or a talented and dedicated artist from an attention-hungry lunatic (a phenomenon that had been solely unique to Chris back in the eighties). Jimmy Kimmel, Jon Stewart, and Stephen Colbert became the pied pipers for this new audience of voyeur/performers, and not surprisingly the younger fans and the new entertainers began to lose touch with the true roots of their shared, comic family tree.

This was a natural evolution, of course, and not necessarily a bad thing for Chris Elliott. It meant that everything old could be new again—if repackaged in the right way. Yet in order for Elliott not to drown in the tidal wave of edgier comedy, he would have to be rediscovered, and although he didn't know it at the time, the stage (at Madison Square Garden, as it turned out) was already being set for such a renaissance.

* * *

In the fall of 2009, Elton John performed three concerts at the Garden. On the third night, he stopped the proceedings halfway through to address the crowd:

"Ladies and gentlemen, seeing how it's Thanksgiving and all, I thought it would be nice to invite somebody up here onstage with me whom you haven't seen for a while. So please join me in welcoming my old friend Mr. Chris Elliott!"

The two had met years earlier in Las Vegas. Elton John was doing his famous Red Piano review at Caesars and Elliott was over at the Mirage playing Bobo the Clown in "Love," Cirque du Soleil's multimedia tribute to the Beatles. Exactly what a clown hanging upside down by a bungee cord had to do with the Beatles is still unclear, but the two struck up a close relationship nonetheless.

Madison Square Garden shook with excitement when New York's hometown boy joined Elton onstage. Although Elliott had been absent from the public scene for a couple of years now, the middle-of-the-road crowd welcomed him back in grand style. He now appeared leaner and a bit older, but still full of the same old Chrissie wee and pee—which he had bottled back in the 1800s, during his Thwacker investigation, and made a fortune selling as a miraculous liniment that he claimed would "cure all that distresses the female disposition" (luckily, he always made it back to the time portal before the turn-of-the-century lynching mobs could catch up with him).

"How you all doing out there tonight?" he asked as he adjusted the microphone, and the crowd chanted back in unison, "We're all doing fine, Mr. Elliott. And how are *you*?"

"I'm fine too," Chris replied. "Thank you for asking. We're gonna do a little oldie for you now," Chris continued. "I just hope I remember how it goes. You all probably know it better than I do." And he counted off, "A one, two, three, four . . ."

The moment Elton John hit the first idiosyncratic piano chords of "Alley Cat," the audience went absolutely berserk. Then, when Elliott began to shuffle around a pile of bananas, it went even berserker. It had been at least twenty years since he had last danced the Banana Dance, and his performance that night electrified the Garden. This of course was due to the massive squirrel drop that replaced the customary balloon drop (Elliott had learned a few tricks from Resnick).

Backstage, Chris was flying high. "Did you hear the crowd, Elton?" he said. "They love me! They still really love me!"

"Yes, I heard them," Elton replied, fatherly. "And somebody else still loves you, too, son."

Chris turned around to see Sweet Paula standing there. It was like love at first sight all over again. Sweet Paula's eyes filled with tears, and Chris's eyes filled with blood.

Unbeknownst to Chris, Elton had invited Sweet Paula to the show that night, and she had been seated front row center watching him wow the throng with his sexy, middle-aged moves. Elton gambled that if she saw Chris again, she might forgive the past, and there might be a reconciliation. He was right. As she watched her estranged husband make a complete idiot out of himself just like he had in the old days, Sweet Paula's mind drifted back to the first time they had met in the elevator at 30 Rock, when his breath smelled so bad, and the time he sketched her portrait as she posed naked except for the corncob pipe in her mouth on the red velvet settee in their private cabin aboard a doomed replica of the *Titanic*, and the time Chris gave up their firstborn child to Garson Kanin's coven of witches in exchange for a guaranteed appearance on *Hollywood Squares*. Her emotions were reignited, and she knew it was time for a cease-fire.

The world around them stopped as their lips met, and they gave each other a tonguey smooch for like twenty minutes. Elton just smiled—Cupid's scheme had worked. Then he got a little grossed out.

"So . . ." Chris said, when the feeling had finally returned to his lips, "how ya been?"

"Good, good," Sweet Paula replied.

"And the twins?" Chris inquired.

"Terrific. They're twenty-one and twenty-three now."

"Jeez, they grow up so fast, don't they?"

"Yeah, especially when you only have two hundred pages to tell your whole life story."

"Right, right, so true. Would that I had another four hundred pages, then I could really get into some tedious minutiae, like our kids—oh well, next time."

Then Chris put his hands on her shoulders and spoke from his heart. "Sweet Paula, I speak from my heart when I say that things are going to be different from now on. You and the twins are my only priority in life. I promise I'll never be seduced by the dark side of show business again. I just want to be a house dad and sit on the sofa and get stoned and watch the wheels go round and round. I'm done with fame and fortune. That stuff is for lousy bums and mother-grubbers. You mean more to me than any creamy broad or two-dollar hooker, or TV show with a million-dollar paycheck!"

"You mean it?"

"You bet your sweet bippy, I mean it. Now let's go home and do the nasty, the old-fashioned way—by bumping uglies with our naughty bits."

As they turned to leave, a timid voice called out, "Mr. Elliott, could we have a word with you?"

Three young men, each wearing Homer Simpson T-shirts and Steve Martin arrows, blocked their exit.

"Yuck," Elliott grumbled. "Comedy writers."

Michael Koman, Andrew Weinberg, and Jason Woliner (the one with the timid voice) were in town to try out actors for *Eagleheart*, a fifteen-minute show that they had just sold to the newly formed cable network known as Adult Swim. Conan O'Brien was set to produce, and they were looking for a Chuck Norris type to play the lead. They had grown up on *Get a Life*, *There's Something About Mary*, and *Dance Flick*, and believed it was time to introduce Elliott's special brand of laughless humor to a whole new generation of suckers.

"Would you be interested in doing a show with us?" Woliner asked. "We're all huge fans of yours."

Elliott was humbled.

"Well, I don't know, boys," he replied. "See, I just kind of gave up show business forever, and I—"

"We have a jet fueled and ready to leave at your earliest convenience," declared a voice laced with an Irish brogue, and Elliott turned to see Conan O'Brien flanked by a couple members of the Fruit of Islam. He was holding out a contract and a check for one million dollars.

Chris swallowed hard. It was the old story—Hollywood was seducing one of its own again. He glanced back at Sweet Paula to gauge her reaction to this new development. It was hard to tell.

"Er . . . honey," he began, "I know I just said I was giving up show business forever, but . . ."

She pressed her finger to his lips. "Shhh," then kissed him softly and whispered in his ear, "Just do me one favor this time."

"What?"

"Get good ratings!"

Chris beamed, and Sweet Paula kissed him again. "Now go get

'em, tiger!" Elton played the theme to *Rocky* on his kazoo, and Elliott signed the contract and took the check.

So once more into the breach—though perhaps this would end up being his final battle, his last hurrah. Like in the days of yore, he was whisked off to Hollywood, and Sweet Paula was once again left behind on the tarmac, but she didn't seem to mind anymore.

"It's just like old times!" she happily proclaimed as she popped her head out of the duffel bag to watch Chris's plane disappear into the clouds.

"Good-bye, my one true love," she voiced softly. "The twins and I shall be waiting anxiously for your return."

She had no way of knowing it then, but it would be the last time she would ever see him alive.

*   *   *

Eagleheart premiered at midnight, February 3, 2011, and was an immediate hit, pulling in huge ratings for the fledgling Adult Swim network. It was ranked the number one fifteen-minute, late-night cable sitcom, winning the key 18-to-49 demographics, and making it clear that the Chris Elliott renaissance was well under way. After a lifetime spent struggling for recognition, now at age fifty, Elliott had been rediscovered by a whole new generation of viewers who luckily had no memory of any of his past work.

The night of March 10, Shelley Winters threw a big party at the Chateau Marmont in honor of Elliott's thirty years in show business. She rented out the entire penthouse suite, which had a perfect view of the massive *Eagleheart* billboard over Sunset Boulevard, on which was emblazoned Elliott's huge smiling face, complete with oversized blackheads, giant pimples, and a bunch of disgusting broken blood vessels.

Just about everyone who had ever played some small role in Elliott's life was there—at least the ones who were still alive or not in prison. Pee-Wee Herman and Pauly Shore, Weird Al and Francis Ford Coppola, Ryan O'Neal, Sir Alfred Molina, Dr. Ruth Westheimer, the Ghoul, the Farrelly brothers, Rona Barrett, Elinor Donahue, Lee Radziwill, Dave Letterman, John Gotti and the boys from the Ravenite Social Club, plus a bunch of pals from the old neighborhood whom Shelley Winters had flown out to surprise Chris—like Old Man Koratzanis, the real-life Conspiracy Guy, and Old Man Angelini, the original Panicky Guy. (The real-life Guy Under the Streets had died tragically a year earlier when a gas leak blew off his manhole cover and his head at the same time.)

"I wish you were here," Chris shouted into the phone, in the bedroom of the penthouse suite. The noise of the party was deafening.

"That's your life, not mine, but I'm happy for you," Sweet Paula replied.

"What are you up to?" Chris asked.

"Oh, just playing Scrabble with the twins and reading your fan mail."

"Am I getting fan mail again? I must really be back on top."

"Well, it's actually another one of those threatening notes, like you used to get from Andy Kaufman."

Chris laughed. "Just like the good old days. Who wants to kill me this time?"

"Someone claiming to be Dr. Adler."

"The renowned Elliottologist?"

"She says you've 'spurned her advances' for the last time."

"Ha, maybe she wants to give me a book deal or something. . . ."

"She goes on to say that she 'hopes you enjoy tonight's party, lard-o, because it'll be your last.'"

"Well, then I guess I better hurry up and get back to the fun before I get murdered."

"Just promise me you'll be careful, all right?"

"Sure thing, whatever. Bye, sweetie."

Little did Sweet Paula know that it would be the second-to-last time she would ever speak to him alive.

Elliott partied hard into the night. Witnesses say he was back on the sauce—tartar, that is. He was definitely hopped up on something because he danced every dance with an inexhaustible oomph. Perhaps he was celebrating the completion of life's puzzle. All the pieces seemed to be in place now, and after struggling for so long to get it right, perhaps he felt he deserved a real blowout, but then again he could have just been drunk. "I think he had one too many tartar poppers," Elinor Donahue observed. "He was really out of it—I mean crunched, blotto, dipso, boiled as an owl, if you'll pardon my French."

At midnight, Winters brought out a big cake, and everybody sang "For He's a Jolly Good Fellow." None of the revelers realized that it would be the last time they would ever sing "For He's a Jolly Good Fellow" to Chris Elliott alive.

Back at the Bram, Sweet Paula had put the twins to bed and was now relaxing with a glass of wine on the living room floor. She was casually creating words out of the scattered Scrabble pieces spread out before her, but her thoughts kept creeping back to that threatening note. Elliott had received many like it over the decades, but there was something about this particular one that didn't sit right. Why was it signed "Dr. Adler"? And what the hell was an Elliottologist, anyway?

At the Chateau Marmont, Michael Stipe was singing a soupy version of "Stand," Dave Letterman was off by himself in a corner doing the Frug, and Elliott was finally showing signs of fatigue. He wandered out to the balcony to get a breath of fresh air and to have a moment by himself. As he stood there, sipping his schnapps, he gazed intently at his colossal face over Sunset Boulevard, reflecting on his turbulent life and career. A sense of melancholy filled his soul.

"All these people are here for *you*," Jim Bailey observed, joining Chris on the balcony. Shelley Winters had flown Jim out to stand in for Sam Elliott, who couldn't make the party because he was shooting a commercial for testosterone supplements. "How does that make you feel?"

"Terrific," Elliott replied sarcastically. "Here's to me."

"What's bothering you, my friend?"

A sardonic smile crossed Elliott's face. "I was just remembering the time Mother told me that 'once you get your name up in lights you can retire from show business. Nothing else matters.' Of course she assumed I'd never have that experience, and yet there it is." He took a sip of schnapps. "It's funny, isn't it, Jim? After everything I went through to get here, and she's not even around to see it. Sometimes I think I did it all for her."

"Well, son," Jim said, putting a hand on Chris's shoulder and sounding eerily like Sam Elliott, "I bet ya she's up there in that big whorehouse in the sky looking down on your ugly mug right now. And I bet I know exactly what she's saying, too." Then he switched voices and sounded even more eerily like Bette Davis. "I may have been hard on the boy, but it was all for his own good. I was just trying to make him a better man, and I believe I succeeded—after all, I couldn't have made him any worse now, could I?"

Chris thought about it for a moment, the warm Santa Ana wind blowing through the solitary blond wisp on top of his tiny head, and then he downed his schnapps and in one swift move threw the glass at the billboard. It smashed to pieces right on the three giant nose hairs that the artist had seen fit to include.

"It is accomplished," Elliott muttered, and, satisfied with himself, turned and headed back into the party.

Jim watched him go, circling his ear with his finger. "Cuckoo!"

At that very moment back in New York City, Sweet Paula had spelled out "Dr. Adler" and was now moving the Scrabble letters around to explore other possibilities. First she formed:

DRADLER

Then, by discarding the L and one of the Rs, she got:

DREAD

She dropped the other R and came up with:

DEAD

"Dead?" she said out loud. The word and all its sinister implications made her uneasy. She moved to the bookshelf and pulled down one of her many copies of the *National Directory of Psychiatrists* (a wedding gift duplicated by several guests). Thumbing through the As she came to Adler, and read out loud, "Dr. Amelia

Adler, noted Sorbonne-trained psychiatrist and sex therapist. Born 1865, died 1920." She stopped. "Died? Dr. Adler is dead?" And then she continued to read: "Dr. Adler is survived by her one daughter, Drew Heresmit Adler, considered to be a dangerous psychopath, who recently escaped from the Karlstadt Institute for the Criminally Insane."

She gasped and put the book down. "Dangerous psychopath," she repeated. "That doesn't sound good." Back on the floor with her Scrabble pieces, she spelled out "Drew Heresmit," and sipping her wine, she furrowed her brow and studied the name. Again she began to rearrange letters. First she came up with:

DREST HEIR MEW

That made no sense, and she sighed—frustrated—but she tried again:

REDS HERMIT WE

"Silly," she said to herself. "That's not even a name. I think I've had quite enough of this, thank you very much." The exercise was getting her nowhere, and she was so discouraged that she was about to call it quits, when she narrowed her eyes on the letters one last time. Slowly, she began to see an order to the chaos. First she saw:

RD

"No, that's not right."

DR

"That's it." Then:

HEIMER

Then:

WESTDRHEIMER

"No, no, it's still not right. I need to move the DR . . ." and then finally . . .

"Oh my God!" she gasped as the hair on her arms stood up on end. "It can't be true! *She's* Drew Heresmit Adler? Dr. Amelia Adler's daughter? And she's insane! *And* she's at the party at the Chateau Marmont! *And* she wants to kill Chris! I have to warn him!"

She immediately picked up the phone and dialed the Chateau.

At that moment in Hollywood, the raucous celebration was in full swing. The Velvet Underground's "Heroin" painted the background noise with a psychedelic overtone. There was no way anyone could have possibly heard the phone ringing or even located it. And even if they had, it just would have been dripping or turning into a giant millipede smoking a Sherlock Holmes pipe.

For Chris, everything moved in slow motion as he meandered through the crowd, heading for the suite's master bedroom. He was tired, certainly, but there was something else—he exuded an air of finality. He seemed somehow finished, finished with the party, finished with his career, finished with everything—perhaps even finished with his life?

"Chris Elliott, where you going?" Jason Woliner's voice sounded modulated and far away—but still meek.

"Nowhere, man," Chris answered. "I've never been going any-where."

"Come with us, man," Woliner pleaded. "These people are vampires."

"Yeah, it's not our scene," Andrew Weinberg added, throwing his arm around Elliott. "Let's blow this joint."

And then Michael Koman joined in. "Yeah, come on, man. Let's ride the snake. All for one and one for all."

"No!" Chris snapped. "I'm not one of you! Don't you get it? I'm too old! Just too damn old!" Then, looking at the young writers' worried faces, he softened a little. "And I'm too tired. I'm going to bed, guys. See you later."

Woliner, Weinberg, and Koman watched Elliott float into the master bedroom and close the door behind him. Little did they know it would be the last time they would ever see him feeling sorry for himself alive.

The bedroom was pitch-black.

Chris was exhausted and it didn't take long for him to begin to drift off.

But then . . .

"Remember me?"

What was that? Was someone else in the room?

He was in that limbo state between reality and the dream world, but he was certain he had heard a voice.

"I said, do you remember me?" It was a woman's voice—a woman with a heavy German accent.

"Who's there?" Elliott asked, blinking himself awake and trying to adjust his sight to the inky universe surrounding him.

"How about the first time you did 'The Guy Under the Seats'? You remember that?"

Whenever the woman spoke, her voice seemed to come from a different part of the bedroom. Elliott reached over and fumbled to turn on the light, but the cord had been cut. He found his flip phone on the nightstand and opened it. The screen lit up and he pointed it around like a flashlight. The ominous shadows in the room looked like Conrad Hall's stark black-and-white footage from *In Cold Blood*.

"Remember that quick little 'knee-knocker' under the bleachers?" the voice asked. The woman sounded like she was on Chris's right side, and he quickly pointed his phone in that direction, but nobody was there—just a sinister-looking palm plant.

A high-pitched old-lady giggle came from the other side of the room.

Again he pointed his phone, but again nobody was there—only a painting of a menacing clown.

"Do you know who I am now?" the voice asked.

"Jesus Christ, how would I know?" Elliott responded nervously. "That was more than twenty years ago. I was banging anything that wasn't nailed down back then. It didn't mean anything to me."

"Well, maybe it meant something to me, hee hee hee. Did you ever think of that?"

"No, of course not! I don't think about other people. I just think about myself."

The cell phone's battery was running low, and the screen's light began to flicker, adding a scary strobe effect to the room.

"You use other people, then?" the voice questioned from some other corner.

"Yes, yes, I use other people. I always have."

"Interesting. Talk about that."

Chris huffed. "Come on, what are you, a shrink?"

"Hee hee hee, maybe I am. Maybe I am." Then the voice grew intimidating. "I said, talk about it!"

"What do you want from me? I've spent my life faking it—using other people and taking credit for their talent. I'm a fake, a loser, a real bum. I admit it. I take and I take and I take, and even when I give back, it's all pretend—just smoke and mirrors. What else do you want me to say?"

"How 'bout 'I'm sorry'?"

"Will that get you out of my room?"

"Maybe."

"Fine. I'm sorry. I apologize to all my fans. I apologize to my friends and family. You've all been duped, but none of you will ever have to hear from me again. I got my billboard. I'll go away now."

The room fell silent.

Elliott squinted, still trying to nail the position of the intruder.

"Hello?" he said.

All quiet.

"Are you there?"

The strobe effect slowed down.

Did that shadow just move?

He tapped his phone but a moment later the light faded out completely, and the room was pitch-black again. He could barely breathe now, and the sound of his heartbeat reverberated in his head.

"Was that good enough? Is that what you wanted me to say?" he asked. "Talk to me, damn it! Have I redeemed myself? Was that good enough?"

The voice whispered in his ear.

"Saying you're sorry is never good enough."

"Huh?"

For a split second the cell phone popped back on, illuminating the knotted face of Dr. Ruth Westheimer hovering over him, holding a giant carving knife.

"Say good night, *Arschloch*!" she snarled.

"I don't know what that means!"

"It means 'asshole,' *Arschloch*!" and then she screamed a horrifying, earsplitting scream and plunged her knife into his chest.

Elliott could feel the blade crack his rib cage and pierce his lung. He gasped for air.

"Why? Why?" he sputtered.

"Because I love you!" Dr. Ruth shrieked, and in a crazed frenzy began stabbing him over and over again. Elliott screamed a horrifying, earsplitting scream of his own.

"Mr. Chris? Mr. Chris?" another voice said. "You all right?"

He continued to scream.

Consuelo Saldar, the Chateau's maid, turned on the bedroom light, but it took Elliott a full minute before he finally stopped screaming.

"Mr. Chris, you all right?" Consuelo repeated.

He was sweating and out of breath. He looked around the room—there was no Dr. Ruth anywhere. He frantically felt his chest—there was no blood, and no knife sticking out of it.

He swallowed air to catch his breath. "Yes, yes, Consuelo," he finally sputtered. "I just had a bad dream. I'm all right. What time is it?"

"Three-thirty in morning," Consuelo replied. "Party over a long
time ago. I'm just straightening up living room. You sleep now?"

"Yes, I'm going back to sleep now. Thank you, Consuelo."

The maid closed the door. She didn't know it then, but it would
be the last time she would ever close that door while Chris was
still alive.

However, phone records indicate that Elliott didn't go right back
to sleep. He called Sweet Paula at the Bram at approximately 3:35 a.m.
and woke her up.

"He asked me if I had put a curse on him," Sweet Paula recounted,
"and then he said that Dr. Ruth Westheimer was mad at him because
of some knee-knocker back in the eighties, and that she was floating
around his room with a knife. I just assumed he had eaten a bad
clam or something and told him to go back to bed, and hung up.
Little did I know that it would *absolutely* be the last time I would ever
speak to him—I promise. In fact, just to make sure, I took my phone
off the hook."

The various accounts of what followed next remain baffling and
contradictory at best, and sinister and criminal with a haze of conspiracy at worst.

Particularly troubling is the timeline of events:

Consuelo Saldar claimed to check in on Chris several more times
during the night (which meant that she actually *did* close that door
again. Why would she lie about that?), and despite the fact that he
had not moved at all, Consuelo just assumed that he was sleeping.
She also told investigators that there were strange people coming
and going in and out of the bedroom all through the night.

At 4:15 a.m. or thereabouts, witnesses saw a helicopter emblazoned with the congressional seal land on the roof of the Chateau. Nancy Pelosi emerged and hurried into the penthouse. A few moments later she reemerged holding what appeared to be Chris's underpants. She got back in the helicopter and took off.

At approximately 4:45 a.m., another helicopter landed, this time emblazoned with the *Ripley's Believe it or Not* logo, and out got two men in dark suits who rushed into the penthouse only to emerge moments later carrying Elliott's beard.

At 4:55 a.m., Hofbräuhaus of Beverly Hills delivered two orders of knockwurst and schnitzel to the penthouse—a woman's voice told the delivery guy to slide the food under the bedroom door. The delivery guy said the voice sounded like a man pretending to be a woman—in fact, he said, it sounded like Chris Elliott pretending to be a woman.

It was still dark out at about five a.m., when Consuelo says she heard Elliott shout, "Help me, Consuelo, help me. They're killing me!" but she thought he was joking and shouted back, "Oh, Mr. Chris, you're such a card! Now stop bothering me. I still have cleaning up to do."

Not long after that, the ghostly apparitions of Peter Lawford and Bobby Kennedy were observed by members of the *Ghost Hunters* show from Rhode Island, who happened to be filming an episode at the Chateau that night. Lawford told the ghost hunters that he and Bobby were looking for a diary that might implicate "Jack" (whoever that was) and said they should mind their own business if they knew what was good for them. "We were never here, understand?" Lawford said, and then he bummed a cigarette and disappeared.

Finding Elliott unresponsive at six a.m., Consuelo finally called his personal physician, and ten minutes later Dr. Conrad Murray arrived, accompanied by three strippers. Murray claimed to have checked Elliott's vital signs, and he told investigators that at that point everything was okay, so after administering an IV of mayonnaise, Tabasco, and Anbesol—a powerful cold sore remedy—he left.

Elliott had still not moved a week later, and he was starting to smell, so Consuelo called the police, who made the grisly discovery. Forensic photos indicate that he was found lying facedown on his bed, stark naked except for the platinum blond Fancy Lad wig from *Cabin Boy* that sat slightly askew on top of his head. The photos also show that his bed was littered with empty schnapps nips and empty jars of tartar sauce—oh, and he also had a ball in his mouth for some god-awful reason.

And that was it.

The bright flame that once blazed across our collective consciousness was finally extinguished. It was, in the words of Charlie Rose, "an obscenely indecorous ending to such an illustrious, ahem, career."

No suicide note was ever found, so we may never know exactly what Elliott felt and thought in those final hours of his life, but luckily this autobiography was left on his nightstand, handwritten on a stack of napkins, which Swifty Lazar immediately sent to David Rosenthal over at Blue Rider Press . . . so actually we do have a pretty good idea of what Elliott felt and thought in his final hours of life—and all through his life, for that matter, and I think we're all the better for it, too, don't you?

To this day, the actual cause of death remains a mystery. But there are those who say that Elliott was simply tired of the charade—that he was done with pretending to be somebody that he wasn't, and that the only thing real for him anymore was death. He had soared high on borrowed wings, especially the wings of the fake Adam Resnick or whatever the guy's real name was, but dying was something he would have to do by himself, and perhaps at least he had accomplished that much—although, as Rona Barrett so aptly put it in her warm, heartfelt eulogy: "He went out like the fink he was. Some dramatic death scene, give me a break—he just ripped off both Monroe *and* Belushi."

Still, Elliott's unique contribution to the world of comedy cannot be ignored. Whether he knew what he was doing or not, he showed us all that comedy doesn't always have to be funny to be entertaining. In fact, it doesn't even have to be entertaining at all.

His audience knew that, and his die-hard fans, perhaps dwindled now in numbers, would always hold him close in their hearts and minds. As word of his demise spread, a handful gathered in the rain at the entrance of the Chateau Marmont. Even in death, his public wanted to be with him, perhaps even more than when he was alive. Their devotion was a sign of just how intimately he had touched each and every one of their lives, and how they would never, ever forget who he was, and what he stood for.

As the body was brought out, one of the paramedics asked his partner, "Who's the guy under the sheets?"

"Oh, you know. What's-his-name. The guy who wasn't funny."

EPILOGUE

It may never be possible to truly assess Chris Elliott's impact on the world of comedy. Was he a charismatic pioneer redefining the boundaries of the human experience through offbeat, avant-garde humor, or just an egomaniacal idiot savant who stumbled blindly through a temporary loophole in our collective notions of "talent" and "appeal"? Will we ever really know for sure? Will we ever even care?

At the memorial service, held March 3, 2012, at the Harlequin Rehearsal Studios in Times Square, Elliott's friends and family and victims wrestled with such questions as they struggled to eulogize him. Sally Jenkins took to the podium first: "I guess I was his first girlfriend, although I didn't know it until somebody named Rosenthal from Blue Rider called to warn me that that's what's gonna be in this stupid book and that I didn't have a leg to stand on if I wanted to sue. To be honest, all I remember about Elliott was that his hips blended into his stomach, his ass blended into his back, and his neck blended into his face. Basically he looked like a walking pinworm. Thank you for listening."

Garson Kanin (then a hundred and one years old) took the microphone next and tried to sum up Elliott's life in a nutshell. "Is this on? Shaba-shaba-doo. Remember that one?" He paused to cough, before continuing, "In 1920-something, I was working at the old Nederlander Theatre down there on Forty-ninth Street, and— No, wait, Forty-eighth Street, no, Forty-seventh Street, no, it was either Forty-sixth or Forty-fifth . . . or . . . Forty-one . . . Forty-two, did you say? Anyway, it was in a burlesque show called *Sugar My Tits*, no, um . . . what the hell . . . *Sugar My Coffee*—that's not it, either—it was *Give Me My Cream, and I'll Give Ya Some Sugar*, er, something like that. *Give 'Em Cream!* That was it! No, it wasn't. Anyway, there was a little bit of a tune in that show called 'Toostie Roll Sweets,' or 'Tootsie Diamond Sweets'—and if I sing a little you'll know why it always made Ruthy Gordon and me think about our dear friend Chrissie Elliott. How the hell did it go again?" He attempted to sing. "'Tootsie for yooz and Tootsie's for me . . . stick 'em in your tootsies and see, dee, dee, dee, with six you get three, banga bee, yabadee, something, something, pumpernickel is free. Weeee . . .' I got a million of those, folks. Oh Christ, I shit myself." A moment later he was gently escorted back to his seat.

Next up was a freakishly tall man with a Ned Beatty tattoo clearly visible on his forearm. You could hear a pin drop as he stood there struggling to hold back tears. "My name is Adam Milosovich Resnick," he said, "and I was Chris Elliott's *real* best friend." Apparently the experimental treatments in Russia hadn't worked, as he now stood about fifteen feet tall. "We were from different walks of life, but I never met anybody who was more like me, except for his height, nationality, financials, religious affiliation, sense of humor, and basic intelligence, but other than that we were like twins—a real team. We were like yin and yang. He was my Lily Tomlin and I his Jane Wagner. . . ." Here Resnick started to break down. "I'm gonna miss ya, kid. It's not going to be easy. We lost a great one with you, but I take solace in knowing that tonight every lightbulb in heaven has a little piece of cheese on it."

David Letterman was probably the most eloquent: "My, oh my, we're having some fun now, aren't we? You know, like so many underrated talents before him—John Bunny, Jimmy Finlayson, and Fatty Arbuckle—Chris Elliott blazed across our collective psyches and then was gone before we had a chance to tell him to stop. But the one difference between Elliott and those other guys, besides a huge deficit in the talent department, is that we'll never really remember him, and if we do we'll probably just get him mixed up with that guy from *Home Alone*. In fact, after this little mishegas here today, I for one don't plan on ever mentioning his name again. Talking about Elliott in the future would just be meaningless busywork. And if I know Elliott, I think that's exactly the way he would want it. Thank you. Good night and drive safely. Pants."

For most of his fans, the memorial service seemed to tie a nice little bow around the pretty package of Chris Elliott's life. But for those obsessive basement cases who just can't let things go, there were the many rumors that persist to this day, like the one that says that he wasn't really dead when the maid found him, but rather just in a state of extreme hibernation—a self-induced trance, if you will. His extensive knowledge of the occult, Vodun philosophy, and his ability to hold his breath for long periods of time, especially under-water (thanks to Bette's bathtub training), is what makes this theory even the slightest bit plausible. Many die-hard believers go so far as to say that the power of Elliott's rigorously trained spirit allowed him to regenerate an entirely new poor excuse for a body. Strange sight-ings, although never substantiated, seem to support the theory. Every Tuesday, a heavyset bald man with a long gray beard sits by himself at LA's Daily Grill, on Ventura Boulevard and Laurel Canyon, always ordering the same thing—the Donald Duck special off the kids' menu, Salisbury steak, mashed potatoes, and peas, with an extra dol-lop of tartar sauce and a child-sized mug of root beer schnapps. But when asked if he's Chris Elliott, he only cryptically replies, "Yes," and then adds, "But don't tell anybody, because it'll screw up the insur-ance for my wife."

And then there's that mysterious woman dressed entirely in black, her face obscured by a veil, who regularly visits Elliott's tomb at Forest Lawn, always leaving behind a single Gitane. Some say it's obviously a man, and in fact that it looks a lot like Chris Elliott in drag, and apparently if you ask her if she's really Chris Elliott, she says, "Yes, but don't tell anyone, because Sweet Paula just bought a speedboat and she'd be heartbroken if it got repossessed."

In the fall of 2012, The Comedy Store held a benefit to cure plan-tar warts and SHS (smelly hair syndrome—the two causes closest to Elliott's heart). It was billed, oddly enough, as "An Evening with Marlon." As the hour approached, speculation ran high—would it really be Chris? Is this how he would make his big comeback, ap-pearing out of the blue to tell us all that it had just been a big practi-cal joke? The Adam Resnick impostor, whom insiders knew had always been the one under that heavy Brando makeup, had gone missing some years earlier, so if not Chris himself, then who could it be? Everyone sat eagerly waiting. But unfortunately that night Michael Richards was first up and he cleared the place out with another one of his charming racist tirades, so Marlon never made an appearance, and the mystery went unsolved.

Perhaps the strangest rumor of all, however, is the one that claims that it wasn't even Chris Elliott who faked Chris Elliott's death. Yes, *someone* died, but it wasn't him. There are those who believe that just like his dad Sam, Chris began using look-alikes sometime back when he was still at the Letterman show. Fearing that he wouldn't be able to handle the pressures and rigors that even a moderately successful career in show business would demand, Chris quietly slipped into the shadows, and it was in fact his doppelgänger who went on to star in *Get a Life*, *Cabin Boy*, and *Eagleheart*, and it was his doppelgänger who married Sweet Paula and fathered Sweet Abby and Sweet Bridey, and it was this person, not Elliott, who met his maker in that bedroom at the Chateau Marmont. It's a tantalizing tale, and if true it would mean that there were really two fakers up there in the Temescal Canyon that night. It would also mean that actually the Chris Elliott impostor killed the Adam Resnick impostor. (And this book was about *who* then, exactly? And for that matter, who wrote it? And who's writing this sentence right now? I'm so fucking confused.)

But in the end it really doesn't matter, because if you think about it (but not that hard), nobody is who they say they are in show business. Everybody dyes their hair, everybody shaves a year or two off their age, and everybody makes up a lot of bullshit when they write their stupid autobiographies. But for fans it might be a comforting thought. As for me, I like to imagine Chris Elliott and Andy Kaufman sunning themselves somewhere far away on a stretch of sandy beach.

I see them drinking daiquiris, banging anything that isn't nailed down (to the sandy beach), and laughing about the big practical joke that we all call this thing called *life*. And then I see Marlon Brando running out of the jungle brandishing his machete. "You insect!" he screams. "Put down that stack of napkins and face me like a man. You defiled my sweet Tarita, and now you will die!" After which he chases Elliott down the beach in jerky over-cranked black-and-white footage, while the Benny Hill theme plays in the background (supplied of course by our friend from the Fox promo department).

ACKNOWLEDGMENTS

I'd like to thank everyone at Blue Rider for all their hard work and dedication to this project, especially Sarah Hochman, my editor, for her patience, guidance, and expert counsel. Thanks also to Associate Publisher Aileen Boyle for navigating publicity and promotion.

Thanks also to my friend Johnny Schmidt for all his valuable assistance, contributions, and unwavering encouragement.

Thanks to my sister, Amy Andersen Elliott, for putting together the fake photo section for me.

And to my agent, David Vigliano, for always being there to miss my phone calls.

And finally, thanks to Adam Resnick, Jason Woliner, Andrew Weinberg, Michael Koman, Jonathan Kimmel, and Jon Schroeder for reading my galleys and putting their valuable two cents in.

PHOTO CREDITS

1. *All About Eve*, Bette Davis, 1950: © 20th Century Fox Licensing/ Merchandising / Everett Collection. Sam Elliott: © 1991 Turner Network Television
3. "Little" Edith Bouvier Beale, circa 1975: © Tom Wargacki / Archive Photos / Getty Images
4. Lee Radziwill, 1960s: Photo by Express Newspapers / Getty Images
5. Saint Valentine's Day Massacre, Chicago, Illinois: Photo by American Stock / Getty Images
6. John Gotti, 1990: © Reuters/Corbis
7. Irving Feinmesser: © Fotosearch.com
8. Robert Wadlow: California State University Archives / Everett Collection
10. © Barbara Gaines
12. *A House Is Not a Home*, Shelley Winters, 1964: Everett Collection
13. *Harold and Maude*, Ruth Gordon, 1971: Everett Collection
14. Rat Pack, *Oceans Eleven*, 1960: © Warner Brothers / Everett Collection. Weird Al Yankovic, 2012: © Barry King / WireImage / Getty Images. Carrot Top, 2011: © James Atoa / Everett Collection. Pauly Shore: Photo by Dimitrios Kambouris / WireImage / Getty Images. Pee-Wee Herman, 1985: © Warner Brothers / Everett Collection
15. Aileen Wuornos: Florida Department of Corrections / Getty Images
16. John Lennon and Yoko Ono: Central Press / Getty Images.

ABOUT THE AUTHOR

Chris Elliott is a comedian and the author of several books, including *The Shroud of the Thwacker*. He has appeared in countless TV shows and films, including *Saturday Night Live, Cabin Boy, Groundhog Day,* and *There's Something About Mary*. He currently stars in Adult Swim's *Eagleheart* and has a recurring role on *How I Met Your Mother*.